Existentialism

and the

Creative Teacher

Existentialism
and the
Creative Teacher

•

Russell A. Peterson
The University of North Dakota

KTH

KENDALL/HUNT PUBLISHING COMPANY
DUBUQUE, IOWA

Printed in the United States of America

Contents

Introduction

In education, the philosophy that must be fundamental is one that will recognize the person, one that will support this person in his efforts for self-development, one that will provide necessary resources, one that will not stifle emerging qualities and one that will be acceptant of the total product developed.

The word education itself supports this notion; from its Latin roots we note its meaning as "to lead out"—to lead out of the person those traits, characteristics and abilities that will make the person or student the unique and distinct individual that he is or wishes to be! To mistake this activity for infusion is to negate the act of drawing out, it is to impose standards, norms or other criteria that develop only pictures, replications of the master. Education is an art; it is not a duplication process. If we use the same criteria for the educator and the process of education that we establish for the artist, that is imagination, creativity, originality, then any form of the art which stereotypes the result to a duplication process will offer but a partial fulfillment of the purpose. There is no doubt that the copyist does produce results that are pleasing to the senses; there is also no question that certain people do relish the product of this activity, but there is also a surety that this "art form" is not to be classed with the work of a Gauguin or a Renoir. This analogy has similar application in education; the "artist-educator" who produces in his work a unique individual cannot be compared to the "artisan-educator" who turns out the "ticky-tacky" conforming stereotype who meets the demands of the world or the society and what they decide to be the educated man. In the latter case, the originality has been distilled out—the essential ingredients allowed to fall by the wayside and be wasted and in its place those expected and desired qualities, that are assumed to be standard, have been infused. Education has not met its goal; it has only prepared another image and set it in its niche in time

vii

to show the world of tomorrow what the general anthropological patterns are today.

Such an approach denies the basic meaning of the word "education!" Such an approach is antithetical to the stated philosophy previously proposed. This approach could be accepted if we were to set our educational philosophy in the thinking of John Locke, with his emphasis on the acquisition of all knowledge; it can be additionally supported in the empirical tradition which offers a finite guide to development and provides only the tangible as normative. Even the pragmatic approach, with its ever-changing concept of truth, its test of acceptance, fails to meet the need for this basic philosophy! The more recent principles stemming from the Vienna Circle have reduced philosophy to a wordy argument, one that could hardly serve as a philosophic base for an educational theory since it would resolve the entire process to a semantic structure or eliminate the facets of the art of education that are based on ethical or metaphysical considerations.

A philosophy that recognizes the dignity of the individual, the uniqueness of the person, the right of free choice can alone be considered as meeting the educational need, and it alone can form the basis for the theories and ideas that must perforce flow from as well as be the well-spring of continued advancement.

If such a philosophy is accepted, it will be found that support of the objectives of education are possible and the further development of the art will follow. But what are the objectives of education? They have been many and varied through the ages. The Greeks looked for physical and mental harmony. The educators up through the Middle Ages sought to develop a thinker along preconceived patterns. The Renaissance educator hoped to develop the "Complete Man." The emphases from this point on have been varied and many, from developing the total man to react within his social structure to creating a computerized automation. In between these extremes there have been rational attempts to meet the needs of the person, but the adherents of this objective have been too few and too silent.

Education must place the person first; it must concern itself with the development of the total person, not in accordance with fixed patterns and designs but rather as the individual sees the need. This is not a throwback to Rousseau, with emphasis on the inherent goodness of youth, it is rather an approach more in concert with Williamson's notion that education will actively provide to the person the direction needed and then permit the individual the right to choose. It will place the decision-making emphasis on the individual; it will offer freedom of choice; it will demand that the person who so commits himself takes the responsibility for this action. This freedom of choice is then not license; it is rather a demand for effectual commitment, commitment in the light of a value system that has been developed in a setting of self-determination and an awareness of the *"other."*

Such an approach may seem, at first glance, to be too *ultra;* it appears to "sever the cord" too early; it seems to put upon the shoulders of a developing individual the onus of saying that the emerging qualities and characteristics of growth and development should be the product of trial and error. Obviously, such a notion, if it were true, would point up the falseness of the approach, because each of the concepts are in contradiction to established psychological principles. But this notion does not imply such defiance; it rather directs attention to the stern demand of self-actualization. It accepts the idea proposed by Karl Jaspers in *The Future of Mankind,* "A small thing. . . .yet a prerequisite of everything else is to think: to look around us, to observe what is going on, to visualize the possibilities, the consequences of events and actions; to clarify the situations in the directions that emerge—until we feel the brutal new fact push our thinking to the very roots of human existence, where the question arises what man is and can be."

The role of the creative teacher can be developed from this position if we accept with Dr. Peterson that "To live critically and responsibly should be the aim of every learner; to achieve this aim is the function of the school, it must recognize the impact of the experiential process." Or as he further states, "The spirit of learning demands that the learner become intimately involved in the process of learning."

From these positions it must be noted that the pressure is on the learner, not the pressure from without, but the stress, the anxiety that Kierkegaard wrote of in *Sickness Unto Death.* It is not the anxiety of despair, but that which stems from the certain knowledge that the individual is faced with the responsibility for his own development, a development that is in harmony with the existence of the "other" and for which each individual must accept the responsibility in its "nowness" as well as its influence on the future choices. This point is again noted by Dr. Peterson when he writes, "To integrate knowledge is to perceive the relationship and responsibility of fact to fact and to bring into focus (actualizing) their associative qualities."

The truly creative teacher is not a demagogue not a martinet, and by the same token he cannot be classed as indulgent or acquiescent. He must be willing to recognize, above all, the worth and dignity of the students; he must provide adequate support for their efforts of self-determination and self-actualization; he must be the resource from whom the student can secure the necessary direction, and he must recognize that, as Dr. Peterson states, "In a sense, education demands more than any one teacher can give, but to find and give direction will always remain his primary task."

Can the teacher whose roots are firmly set in the concrete of positivism and doctrine meet these requirements? It may be possible, but the question appears to be beyond the limits of an acceptable hypothesis. There appears to be only one philosophy that truly supports each separate and distinct notation of these educational demands, and that is a philosophy of education that is based in existentialism. This philosophy demands commitment; it forces recognition of the "other"; it supports the urge for self-determination, and it holds that the individual is responsible for his choices. Within this philosophy there is not the license that permits unconcern, indiscrimination or promiscuity. On the contrary, there is the stern demand for commitment away from hedonism, a requirement that the act of creating the self be the result of decisions made in the light of the actualizing needs of the person and his commitment to his fellow man.

In this work, *Existentialism and the Creative Teacher,* there is a judicious melding of the principles of learning, the concepts of knowledge and their application to the demands of learning as well as the subjective ideas of the existential philosophy. It offers a synthesis of the psychological principles of learning and the theory of knowledge, set against the existential demands placed on the teacher and the learner. This method of treatment is such a radical change from the approaches previously taken and one that examines with such depth the learning process that it should be used as a primer by all educators who hope to bring to the teaching profession the understanding and concern that is demanded of the truly creative teacher.

John T. Wynne

1

The Meaning of Existentialism

1. Definition of Existentialism

For the sake of providing a working definition of existentialism, it will be sufficient for our purpose to suggest that it is that movement within the human mind which exercises its power of transparency to emphasize the responsibility of the will in becoming aware of all factors inherent in the construct of a value condition.

The key-word here is transparency. Transparency and its attributes become the goal towards which the existentialist strives; it is the lodestar of the existential mind. Such a philosophically-oriented mind recognizes that only the real can be perceived and reflect what *is*. What exists is real because of its characteristics, namely, its nature, scope and purpose. What is seen and perceived reveals, in varying degrees, its structure. Transparency is the delineating factor in the relationship between the intellect and its object. The mind learns when it is able to *see through* an existent.

Existentialism places a different emphasis on the learning process than most psychological schools of education. The aim of the learning process, for the existentialist, is to obtain an understanding of the implicative values inherent in every object. Every fact *is* a fact because of its relationship (dependent on its nature) with other facts. This is what we mean by *movement within the mind;* there is an acceptance of the responsibility to see things within a context.

One of the first of these responsibilities is to point out the erroneous belief that entities exist. What exists does so because of its dependency on something else. What is learned comes into being within the mind because of that activity, which through the effort of the will, places a value upon its activities.

The mind functions only because it is not an entity; as it functions, it moves; for the mind to move, it must reflect. Operationally, this is the way the mind works. We must not be deceived in believing, however, that this movement is synonymous with our intellectual

1

activity. It implies much more than *an* intellectual activity. It involves the process of reasoning which brings into existence the *potential* inherent in the learning process. Learning takes place when an existent is perceived within the context of the relationship reflecting the process involving the dependency between cause and caused, caused and causing. All things which exist, including ideas, are the resultants of cause, and by their very nature and purpose, in turn, serve *to cause.*

Existentialism is the science of conceptualization. It has as its subject matter every object which confronts the human mind. It does not limit itself to the thought process alone. Its task is not research, the unveiling of new facts and their relationships. Rather, its aim is the construction of a dialogue the purpose of which is to understand *why* the fact exists in the first place. As a science, it works on principles and their methodologies. Since principles are based on laws, the mind well knows its need for structure. Existentialism is a highly structured determinant; it must draw conclusions, but only when its process of conceptualization permits it to see through an existent.

2. The Perspective of Existentialism

During every moment of its existence, the human mind is being confronted by some object; as a result, the mind finds itself continuously needing to evaluate these confrontations. Evaluation and the value judgment are the two primary functions of existentialism. These are the two factors which provide movement within the human mind. Evaluation is not a matter of affirmation or even denial; it does not establish a dichotomy between subject and object nor does it dispense attributes to things. Evaluation is not an act, suggesting completion. Rather, evaluation is the method whereby, in judging the validity of a relationship, a concept is formed of the inherent value suggested within the dependency construct between facts. Thus, we see the close affirmance between evaluation and the value judgment. There is no pluralism in the process of judgment. There is a deeper inference here, based on the necessity of the value judgment to express a prediction which evolves out of the need for a fact to reveal its inherent dependency factors as the mind probes into its structure to determine the validity of its premises.

3. The Place of Existentialism in the Learning Process

Existentialism includes within its structure the perspective of a speculative science; its purpose is to react, based on the judgment of its evaluative powers, to the evolving process emanating from the relationships of the human mind to everything which confronts it and infers a value.

The fact of existence confronts the mind with *the need to know*. This is the proposition upon which the mind feeds. The need to know, says existentialism, is to remind the mind that the pursuit of knowledge is never for its own sake. Moreover, to search for structure is to look for design, order and meaning. The realization of this existent by the mind is actualized only when the mind moves, by intellect and will, to analyze the construct and purpose of *fact*. This involves one facet of the reasoning process, the result of which must be internalized by the mind.

The science of the reasoning process deals with the relationship between thought and object (or things) and makes no distinction between reality and the mind's concept of it. Its premise is that all things are caused (including ideas) and, because of their existential responsibility, recognize their need *to cause*. This is what existentialism means by the concept *bring into being*. What *is* includes things already a part of the mind as well as those which remain propositions awaiting internalization. To bring into being what exists but has not been internalized by the mind is the responsibility of the learning process.

Existentialism's sole responsibility is with the ability of the mind to rationalize the purpose of an existent. Conceptual modes of thought actualize reality and give meaning to things. Just as all things exist because of the conditions which brought them into being, the process of thought is dependent upon presuppositions to give it direction. Representations do not assure the mind of reality; this is accomplished by means of *relations* alone. Extentialism then, has as its frame of reference the totality of the human being and involves the operative forces of the senses, intellect, will and imagination. It is a regulative science, basing its methodology upon principles which have as their objective the determination of truth. As a regulative science it is concerned with the *form* its thought process must assume in its relationship to reality, the validity of thought as a process, and its dependency upon the conditions found in every proposition.

For the true existentialist, thought and reality are one and the same. What has meaning is brought into being and realized by means of the thought process. Thought is always in the process of development and realizes itself when meaning is discovered in an existent. The implications of this intellectual stance soon become apparent for the teacher in determining his responsibility to the learning process.

The Conceptual Mode of Thought

The human mind soon realizes that meaning, in order to be determined, must first be conceptualized. The process by which this is accomplished is really never completed. Truth is realized only as it is apprehended. This is the proposition which gives structure and perspective to the thought process.

The intellect deals in ideas. To intellectualize means to open the mind to confrontations by ideas, calling forth its methodologies for the apprehension of relationships inherent in every idea. To conceptualize means to think abstractly. Here the mind comes into its own; its concern for detail is now rewarded with an opportunity to move inductively; conceptualization demands a perspective of the whole seen within the construct of its parts. Part is applicable only to a whole. The *concept* insists that the whole is realized when seen in its relation to all parts. This is the meaning of *form* discussed above.

The mind has an insatiable drive to conceptualize; in the process, it conceives ideas. Ideas have a dual nature; they are universal in scope, but particular in meaning. This is true because the mind does not permit entities or segments of thought to remain in isolation, within its areas of learning responsibility. Ideas have a cohesive texture; to live they must unite and form new ideas. They learn from one another. This is what gives them their universal character and intellectual stance.

Unless an idea is abstracted, it cannot be composited and used together with another idea. To intellectualize an idea is to determine its compatability with other ideas; here the imagination is called into play. The object of thought, therefore, is always an idea. The real power of the mind is realized in its ability for abstraction and conceptualization. There is nothing, says the mind, which possesses an independent existence. It is for this reason that the existentialist believes that such a thing as *quality* cannot be considered apart from its referent. Abstraction does not exclude the subject in its consideration of relationships; it knows it is an inherent part of it.

1. Connotative Value

To suggest that the term *characteristic* may be applicable to the concept *connotation* when we are in the process of defining it, is to fail to understand another dimension of the power of the mind.

Knowledge has a way of increasing; it can increase as an article in the knowing process, that is, as a supposed fact and placed in an academic storage bin. In this case, its essence becomes that of a completed act, awaiting display space. Its meaning may be nothing more than the satisfaction gained in mere recognition by the mind of an existent. On the other hand, there is a knowledge purported by the existentialist which says that real knowledge exists only in the mind which understands the nature of the existent being learned. Such knowledge means a recognition of its connotative value has taken place.

To arrive at the connotative value of a fact is to determine the principles underlying its construction; to look at the characteristics of a fact is to look only at externals. Connotative value asks the question *why* in determining meaning *for* and *in* an existent. Meaning implies more that the sum of representations often described by characteristics. In this sense, to determine connotative value is to fill the position in the learning process which calls for a qualifier. This is exactly the responsibility attained by the mind in its search for associative qualities among facts. To conceive ideas using ideas as a base is one of the powers of the intellect. In this process, conception takes place only when meaning is already present and the original idea has associative or connotative value.

2. The Absolute as the Creation of the Real

Since it is the position of the existentialist that all existents are relative in nature (meaning they exist because of inherent relationships) and an absolute is an existent, it is also relative in nature; it is related in the correlative sense. The mind, while it does not *represent* reality, makes it possible for reality to be actualized. In this way, reality and its meaning is both subject and object, neither of which can connote value if studied in isolation. Based on the relevatory powers of each existent, relationships among existents are determined by the mind. To conceive inherent relationships among facts is to conceptualize identity. To identify cause is to determine the intention of an absolute. To conceptualize is to open the real in order to probe into its operative and causative forces. Operative and causative forces are absolute; these forces alone bring reality into being for the learner.

3. The Value Condition

Before an existent can meaningfully be brought into being, the condition upon which its life depends must be validated by the mind. It must be evaluated and the condition which brings it into being ascertained. It is readily apparent, then, that one responsibility of the mind is not assignation. What *exists* does so because of innate qualities and not because of attributes or characteristics assigned to it by the mind. The content of thought, in order for meaning to be found, must be identical with the object of its inquiry, namely, the attribute found only in the quality of an existent.

To exist means the same as *is*. What *is* exists because of the conditions which give it meaning. Quality is always a qualifier and, as such, determines the value of an existent. Truth (meaning) is arrived at or attained when the mind appropriates the quality of a thing and understands its dependencies and relationships to other facts or existents. In other words, the mind via the methodologies of the learning process conforms with the intellectual directives emanating from the relevatory powers of the object of inquiry. Value and its determination is dependent upon the conditioning procedure inherent in the learning process. In reality, value is nothing more than the potentiality of that which is relevant for the mind. The mind does not tell itself what an object *is;* rather, the mind reacts to the substance of a quality, the reaction constituting the essence of the learning process. What exists has being; to determine the essence of being is to determine the meaningfulness of the learning process. Learning is a matter of conceptualization based on the determination of those conditions which give meaning to an existent. We conceptualize only what exists; out of something, something comes into being. To signify the identity of an object is not sufficient justification to say that learning is taking place. To identify quality is to function wholly when the conditions presupposing the relevatory powers of that quality are identified.

The mind does not act; it actualizes the object of its inquiry. To conceptualize is to destroy the myth that entities exist. Truth is found only in the synthesis ordered in judgment. Aristotle said the same thing this way: Truth demands a language, a synthesis of concepts as though they were but one.

Modes of Learning

There is a science of learning not wholly based on methodology. Within its structure are principles, the nature of which suggest their applicative values. They are determinative, therefore operative, and apply to all facets of the learning process.

Learning comes into being when an unknown *becomes* known because the learner experiences its meaning and realizes its applicability to other existents. This is achieved when the material of knowledge (for instance, one fact) is conceptualized in the mind and *ordered* in existence, thereby given a place in the perceptual scheme of the learning pattern. To order a fact is to recognize the working principles behind its condition for existence. To *order* is to relate the fact to what already is known by the mind. This is the process of conceptualization. Moreover, it is the first *mode* of the learning process.

1. The Concept

To conceptualize, the learner must be aware of the requirements of thought and the demands laid down by the mind as it thinks. By nature, the mind relies upon logic in its need for order. There must be an order of thought; ideas build upon ideas, each telescoping into the next, each explicative of the other. It is a matter of one fact affirming the other. As an existent, an idea exists because of its dependency upon other facts. Here again is the question of condition. It is a matter of determining the condition of an existent's *being.*

Why does something exist? is another way of saying what was suggested in the last sentence. It is not enough to suggest everything *is* what it *is.* The existentialist introduces the question *why* into every relationship. Order demonstrates the logic of an existent by means of an analysis of its cause.

2. The Proposition

The first step the existentialist takes in this analysis is dependent upon the proposition; its existence is dependent upon the object which determines it. The proposition is an extension of the thing it seeks to support and project. The relationship between the two is all important; the proposition must be the resultant of the intention of the mind of its determinant.

The task of the proposition is not to quantify; rather, it is to prepare the groundwork for the later process of evaluation and explanation. It has within itself all of the elements necessary for the mental reaction of judgment.

The process giving birth to a proposition recognizes the need to identify all structural facets which comprise the mind of the subject being proferred by means of the proposition. The proposition speaks for its subject, but in doing so, the quantitative aspects of its structure serve to identify its meaning for other objects in relation to itself. The proposition projects the potential *meaningfulness* of that relationship. The responsibility of the proposition lies in its powers of abstract thought; it is a matter of qualification; it explains its subject to another subject. The proposition answers the questions: what are the attributes of a particular subject? and, *why* are they attributes in the first place?

The proposition takes the existence of its subject for granted; thus, its subject is more than an object of thought. In this way the proposition belongs to the conceptual order. This order recognizes the concept as an integral part of existence.

What exists, exists because of the innate implications of its life. To possess the power of abstraction is to identify the implications of an existent. Only the mind actualizes this relationship. By means of the power to abstract, the mind utilizes another dimension of its ability, namely, to bring into being the *potential* of an existent. What is, *is,* but *what* it becomes can be proposed only by the mind in relation to another existent.

The proposition is a mode of bringing into being the potentiality for learning. Learning takes place when meaning is found, when there is an understanding of the existential implications of the object of study. Knowledge is augmented by means of the ability of the intellect to conceptualize.

The conceptual order recognizes that all existents possess antecedents; the task of the mind is to project potential consequences when the original existent is paired with other existents. This is done by means of the proposition.

While the mind is a thing *caused,* its function is *to cause;* while in nature it is dependent upon antecedents, its purpose is to create consequences. Here is order in the process of thought.

3. Inference

At first glance it may seem as though inference is nothing more than a mental act wherein the truth suggested in a proposition is already implied in its antecedent.

Within the proposition lies the potential for the mind to realize the meaning revealed in the structure of an existent. Inference is the third step *reacted upon* by the mind in the learning process toward the apprehension of knowledge. The mind moves within a proposition and it looks for the facts and their relationships which made the proposition possible in the first place; when these have been ascertained, the implications evolving from their relationships structure new concepts, namely, the inference. Here is movement within the mind based on the potentiality of a relationship. The transformation taking place *happens* only in the mind; it is a conceptual expression in reaction to a new relationship established between two existents known by the mind.

4. Definition

Definitions are propositions; as propositions their purpose is the delineation of their own nature. *What* is true in one's nature and *why* is the analysis demanded by a proposition. Only in this way is definition arrived at. To define is to make the nature and essence of an existent transparent. To accomplish this, definitions include more than characteristics. To analyze nature is to describe structure. Characteristics may refer to externals alone; to determine the *why* of structure is to internalize the meaningful relations which undergird all structure. Thus, we come to the concept of *meaning* in a definition.

A definition does not exist if meaning is not present. Meaning is not present without the realization of essence. To exist is to do so *because of* definition, thus, by meaning and essence. Essence is presupposed in existence. The foundation of definition is existence and essence. Characteristics are describable because of essence. To describe essence is to determine structure and find meaning.

The true learner reasons from definitions, therefore, from meaning.

Definitions have the responsibility to uncover purpose. If the definition states the purpose of an existent it is opening the way to an understanding of its nature. The unifying purpose of an existent gives it meaning.

5. Hypothesis

Learning begins when there is confrontation, the presence of a problem. To analyze the problem is to establish a methodology. Methodology is always interested in potentialities of what *might be.* It is at this point that hypotheses are invited into the learning process.

Hypothesis is a cognitive cripple; it cannot stand alone. Because it is a supposition, it is dependent upon other factors to give it existence and determine its relevancy. Hypothesis is *conditioned,* which is the same as saying that its existence is conditioned by those factors upon which it depends for meaning. It has a high ideal, namely, to explain the problem. However, in order for it to serve as a medium of explanation, it realizes that it must first be aware of what is demanded in explanation. *To be able to explain* presupposes that *reasons* have been found which logically interpret an existent. This means the problem has been stated and recognized as such with accompanying implications. Now the questions: *why* is it a problem? *what* makes it a problem? what are the parts in relation to the whole? what are the knowns? the unknowns? are asked. The next step beyond such analysis is experimentation. How are these questions resolved? In what ways? What are some possibilities?

Hypotheses are possibilities. The question is, *when,* at what point in the learning process is the learner *entitled* to suggest possible solutions? First of all, it depends upon what he has discovered about the problem which might suggest potentiality. The learner is always the active participant in the learning process. *While* the material of knowledge reveals external characteristics about itself, the initiative (observation and experiment) rests with the learner. Only the learner possesses the mind. But it is the material of knowledge, the sum total of his problem, which will determine the validity of a supposition. A learning problem has many dependencies. To actualize these is to bring them into being in the mind of the learner. To see their relevancy to the problem is the responsibility of the methodology known as observation. While the material of knowledge possesses revelatory powers, still greater are those powers of insight so necessary to the learner. The most important ingredient of insight is the ability to find the working principles which determine the meaningfulness of relationships between a whole and its parts. To *know* a whole is to *know* its parts in relation to each other; to know one part is to see it in relation to other parts; to know a part is to know the whole in its cognitive perspective. The test of such suppositions is to be found in the meaningfulness of the relationship between parts and the involving of parts with a whole. Here, alone, is the test of truth; to follow such a methodology means a process has been set in motion.

Truth presupposes coherence; wholeness implies the absence of internal contradictions, the realization of *why* certain facts belong together.

What is the method which may bring such realization into being?

6. Method

How do we attain knowledge? How does the human mind actualize essence? At what point in the learning process is the material of knowledge realized by the mind? These are questions which only a philosophy of methodology can answer.

The human mind attains knowledge and its material when a fact (at this point, a supposition) is hypothesized for its potentiality because it possesses the possibility of explanation of some unknown; when this fact becomes something more than a theoretical portent because it exudes meaning by the mind's apprehension of its inherent principles and relationships to other facts, it has moved from a *caused* status to that of *causing* and learning now takes place. To learn is to realize the essence of an existent. This is the same as saying that methodology has as its aim the determination of reason and logic behind every fact. While methodology is concerned with external characteristics of the material of knowledge, its primary concern is with its essence. It is not a cause and effect relationship; it is a cause, causing dependency. It is a process of analysis, movement from problem or confrontation to a determination of relationships and principles. Within the process lies the methodology for the discovery of reasons. From an existent we bring into existence an essence to this point not actualized by the mind. Each fact is an existent; as an existent, it is caused; to give itself meaning it must, in turn, cause learning to take place so as to enable the mind to determine its structural principles and laws of origination.

The mind in process, when confronted with a problem, must determine the methodology necessary for its analysis. Hence, analysis is the mind's solution to the question of methodology. Analysis, as an effective methodology, is dependent upon its powers of synthesization. To become aware of the implications of a network of principles, and synthesize them (to see them in relation to one another) is to move from the realization of *cause* to *caused* to *causing*. To understand the principles of transition in the process is to understand the mind's movement toward the realization of meaning. The mind moves in order to explain.

7. Explanation

Where does the mind begin in order to explain? Before this question is answered, we must first define what it means *to* explain.

The mind stands in a unique position with respect to the concept of explanation. On the one hand, the mind *needs* to find meaning in something not yet comprehended. On the other hand, it is the mind which alone can intellectualize an object to the point of acquiring knowledge, of making the object intelligible. To explain is to render meaning; that is, to permit the mind to experience the unknown in a way that it becomes known.

To explain, the mind must possess the insight necessary to understand essence, therefore the nature, of an existent. What is understood by the mind is revealed by the light provided by the mind.

To explain, the mind sees its object not as an entity but within its own life's context. It is able to determine what factors give the fact life. This means finding its dependencies as well as those facts which depend upon it for life. Here is a dependency upon first principles. The mind finds meaning when it is able to explain *cause*. It is cause and its intellectual attributes which makes explanation possible. This is the same as saying *every fact is conditioned to exist*. Existence implies condition. To understand condition is to understand cause. To determine condition is to bring explanation into the realm of potentiality.

Learning is a matter of being able to explain the relation between the cause and its ability (conditions) to cause. Learning takes place only when the mind organismically determines meaning between a part and its whole.

2

Existentialism and Education

Who is the existentialist?

We first asked the question: what is existentialism? We now ask: who is the existentialist?

In the first place, he is man. As man, he is more than a product of an environment or of a crisis. He is neither alone, unshielded, nor is it necessary for him to be vulgar, obscene or immoral. Above all, he is not his own judge of right and wrong; he well realizes that right and wrong exist, and that restraints are very much a part of life.

In the second place, he is a man who recognizes that the stance of the individual is the most important concern of his existence. This means there is a dual focus, one beam emphasizing the individual and what he can make of himself through finding the meaning of life (for himself and the good of society), and the other, emphasizing the resultant society and what it can mean for the individual. All of which is to say, the existentialist is an individual searching for his true purpose in life, recognizing what an intensely personal thing it really is. He recognizes that he is constantly being influenced and confronted by all aspects of society; but, on the other hand, he is in a position to influence and confront society by decisions which he alone can make.

An existentialist, then, is a man who asks himself the question: how can I meet the demands which confront me every moment of my existence? He is aware of the fact that the *how* of his response will determine the construct of his own potentiality. He is moving on two levels; he must garner his resources to validate the method he is going to use, and he must move, at the same time, toward the realization of his powers of awareness and strength. He asks himself: what are my capacities? This is a question he does not answer by himself. The answers must be drawn from all effective resources at his disposal. How he uses these resources and weighs their directives for

13

him as an individual will determine the meaningfulness of the decisions which he must make.

Choice is a key word in the vocabulary of the existentialist. He is concerned with the question: how does one make a choice and then know that it is the right one?

To do so, the existentialist insists that one of his most important attributes is to be knowledgeable of those things which affect his existence. This means more than being a collector of facts; he must *know* what to do with them after they are collected and how to weigh their validity. This requires a great deal of honesty on his part, an activity necessary in the mental stance of every existentialist.

In the fourth place, the existentialist recognizes the need to look upon himself in his being as an individual, not as an object of study but as the subject of human reaction. He meditates upon himself as a self, recognizing that the objects of his study do not include the self-concept but rather the many alternatives included as an integral part of each confrontation. His task is to envision the results of his choices and guage the effects of his decision upon his thinking; this is the existentialist's mind.

For man to be the subject of personal human reaction is to take it for granted that the self exists; but *how* he exists and *why* changes his relationship to the self. What *is* the self then becomes the most important concern of the individual.

To ask: who am I? and find the answer is to realize that the goal of the individual is to be able to identify with the self. To do this is the supreme task of the existentialist. To accomplish it, the first prerequisite is to recognize within the self a deep obligation to the self and the things which comprise the totality of being. This points out the need for a deep seriousness toward the self; it becomes a *way* of thinking about being. To make such an identification is to be aware of all forces which seek to make an in-road upon the human being. To find out where these forces begin, their intention as well as their force is a part of being knowledgeable about reality. The existentialist is without inherent knowledge at this point until he has found the meaning of essentials.

The existentialist is aware that he has been created as a human being; from this point he becomes the creator of the self, the finisher and qualifier of his existence.

He must answer the question: what does it mean to be created? What does it mean to assume the role of creator and recognize the underlying responsibilities inherent in making a choice? It is done by questioning the meaning of one's own existence, but first *knowing* what it means to exist and what is required by the mind to determine its own validity. This is why Berdyaev said: "I am existentialism. It is only the self who can control the mind and account for its responsibilities."

In what does the existentialist believe?

The existentialist believes in himself, not as a thing but as a self-determining being. Things determine each other. He believes he possesses the freedom of will; he makes himself, but with the assistance of others and things; he has potentiality, the actuality of which depends upon the decisions he makes and not upon the conditions which confront him.

To decide or not, how and why, is the question of the existentialist. Perhaps it is more simple not to act; the existentialist must act responsibly. To make a decision is to take a stand for what one believes in. The failure to make a decision says just as much as making one, says the mind of the existentialist.

Sartre was wrong when he said we are condemned to freedom. It is the task of the existential mind to qualify the conditions of freedom and give it its significance as a qualifier in decision making. It is a question of determining the bases for the morality of an act. This I must choose for the self; others may assist me, but the decision and its responsibilities are mine. To do so means I must decide *what* I believe in and *why*. The existentialist believes he must be committed to his values. But this requires freedom, a creative sort of existent. It might suggest conformity, or it might not. It is in the matter of values the existentialist proves his individuality. It is in the choice of values that he finds the opportunity to find meaning in and for life. Value is life. Freedom provides the setting out of which values evolve. These values, like freedom, exist as a construct of the mind. Meaning is found when value is realized; value is realized only because freedom exercises its responsibilities to the self. Gabriel Marcel put his finger upon this concept when he said: there is no freedom until individuals are able to say "I am I."

This is different from saying, like Sartre, I am responsible for everything, except for my very responsibility, for I am not the foundation for my being.

Not so, says the true existentialist. We are responsible because we are the foundation of our being. *I am because I choose.* Marcel expressed the idea that man is free to make a commitment and then is free to decide whether or not he wants to fulfill this commitment. The more I free myself from the prism of ego-centricism, he says, the more I exist.

The existentialist believes he is a unique creature because of his freedom to choose. Freedom is the opportunity to think and to act freely. When this is realized there is no limit to man's potentiality.

The existentialist believes he exists and has being; he believes he is aware of himself, and by searching for meaning and finding it, can understand himself. He is conscious of the self and by means of this consciousness can experience himself. He experiences himself when he sees the self within a setting, confronted by other individuals and things. He experiences the self when the relationships between the self and 'others' become transparent and he becomes aware of the reasons for his attitudes toward them and the psychological documentations of his actions. He realizes his actions are unique because he is an individual; his mind is unique. To validate the uniqueness of his actions in terms of his potentiality means he has found the meaning of existence.

The existentialist begins with the self and all this implies. From these—the essence of his existence—evolve all thoughts and values; it is more than an intellectual exercise; it is a study in the potentiality of awareness.

The existentialist believes in the priority of the question: *why* am I? From what do I come? From this source is to be found indicators of potentiality. There is a source of potentiality which is mine alone. Only I can actualize it. It possesses me until I can possess it. The finding of *it* is the task of the existentialist. It is what he believes in more than anything else and what he has the responsibility to find and possess that gives him his freedom as an individual. In the process, he becomes more fully aware of what he can be as he continues to be what he is.

What does it mean to be human?

Pervading existential thought is a deep concern that each man recognizes the reality of human dignity. To achieve this, the individual must believe he possesses it within himself and that he has gained it by his use only of the *self* and not at the expense of another. The true existentialist refuses to *use* someone else to fulfill himself; he is convinced of his own human dignity because it is his own, attained only at his own expense.

Thus, the existentialist recognizes that his greatest problem is to know himself. Meaningfully, he cannot know the world of persons and things and understand their implicative values until his studied reactions have affected his experiential constructs. To know himself as an individual means his mind is open to all of the possible confrontations of the morrow; he is aware of the meaningfulness of internal experiences, what is happening around him, as well as those things which may have an effect upon his existence.

The existentialist, in asking what it means to be human, is showing his concern for the deeper levels of existence and experience. He knows it is only the involved self which becomes conscious of the potentiality of the self; this is achieved only as the person experiences himself. This means the individual is no longer comprised of parts, but he recognizes the totality of what *is* the self, a unification of being. This is the existentialist's definition of the involved self as he finds himself as a human being.

The existentialist believes he exists as a man because he possesses the power and insight found in choice. Whatever he does is the result of choice; this is one thing he is unable to escape. It determines his relationship to the self as well as to others; it is the key of his determinative powers of consciousness. It is the key to his control of his *humanity*. The life inherent in humanity is not the *something* given at birth; it is what the individual is willing to make of it. At birth, man is something, but to become more than something *must* become his goal. Man creates his own life and does this by finding meaning in all of existence; he does this by means of *using* the opportunities afforded him in choice.

Existential man does not judge nor condemn the setting or situation in which he finds himself. He does, however, recognize its impact and influence upon him, and, if necessary, will change both. Such a stance changes the complexion of the anxiety in which man so often finds himself. While he often finds the self an anxious being, he knows he must find a replacement for the anxiety. He knows he is something; to move from something to more than something, and recognize the meaning of the word *more* in this context, is to move the self beyond the anguish and destiny of the accompanying despair.

To be human is to recognize the potentiality of choice. This is Kierkegaard's 'either—or.' Man must transcend the depersonalization of the mere 'something' in his life or be destroyed by it. The *mere something* is not enough upon which man can build a self-image. And to think he can escape any part of existence is not a problem; the problem lies in what he brings by way of mental and spiritual ammunition to the confrontation. To determine the validity of these needs is to emphasize the futility of even playing with the concept of escape; no one can escape from the self. Rather, to meet every confrontation ably prepared is his task.

To define human values after these have evolved from man's spiritual stance, points out that he must continue to develop supports for his life. These supports are his ideals; by means of ideals, the existentialist reaches up and out to find meaning for his existence. To experience life is to make of the self what man wills. Man becomes an existentialist when he accepts the responsibility of humanness, that is, the responsibility for giving meaning to life.

It is impossible for man to separate the self from his being; he is always a whole even though it may be meaningless when tried on for size. To ask the question, who am I? is to ask *what* does it mean to be human? Here is the thrust of existentialism. The question is not *how* you answer it, but *with what*. Inherent in the question is the value condition and the value judgment.

Man, then, is more than he is because of the potentiality inherent in humanness. To realize this potentiality is to actualize meaning in life. Man does not need to be the effect of cause. True, he is caused, but here he says, this is as far as I go in being a *product*. "Now, I want to cause." Thus, the existentialist is not an object but the subject of the dialog with the self. It is only this human being who is enabled to experience meaning and recognize it as being synonymous with life.

Who is the individual?

One characteristic which is predominant in the life of the individual is that he is not isolated; he always has himself for a constant companion. To strengthen this relationship and make it meaningful is the task of the existential self. This is the meaning of self-actualization for the existentialist. In order to achieve it, he must be free to understand the nature of his alternatives. He is free to choose, but the attendant consequences are implied in his choice. This idea is closer to the thinking of Jaspers who said we must learn how to die, i.e., make the choice of how we want to die, than to Sartre who tells us that freedom is experienced only in the face of death.

It is the individual who asks such questions as: what meaning does life have for me? what are the ultimates in my life? Each of these questions imply the need to choose from among alternatives. It is by means of the encounter implied in choice that the individual matures and creates those psychological settings from which his values evolve. To discover the potentialities inherent in a value is to realize one's self as an individual. This is saying the same thing as Kierkegaard when he stated that meaningful experience may be equated with growth toward the realization of truth in its wholeness. Life, he said, is a process of choice and decision. The key to the process, however, is to be fully aware of the *why in* the choice and the implicative values *in* the decision. It is only in the meaningfulness of experience that learning takes place.

Freedom and choice, only two words, but both of them significant for the existentialist. An assumption here is a man who is capable of choice; in choice should be the realization of a need to reach out and up for a new and definitive understanding of the self. This is the process of becoming, so important to the existentialist. It is a unique process, allowing the individual to transcend the self, take a look at the self and then decide, by means of his choices, how to actualize his potential. To do this requires the whole being; *becoming* involves the total self. To do this means that as he gathers new facts about himself, they should have only one implicative value, namely, to open new channels of communication with the self in order to envision his own potentiality. We have here another dimension in the matter of choice; it refers to something more than suggesting choice as an act; it is a process. Choice destroys its own nature and perspective when man considers it but an act.

The process of choice recalls the concept of responsibility and requests a definition of scope. The process of choice implies a heavy responsibility for the learner; it suggests the question: how will *the* choice affect the self and others? Here is the control principle of all existential thought. Choice becomes a proposition proffering what a man understands himself to be and want. What he is to become will depend upon the choices he makes because of the *kind* of responsibility he is willing to assume, for himself and for others.

The thrust of Heidegger's thought suggests a question: how aware am I of the responsibility which is mine alone to develop a more mature self?

What is the meaning of authenticity?

What is a mature self? The existentialist believes it is an authentic self.

This is not a play on words. The existentialist posits his belief that man is able to actualize an authentic existence; it is the liberating force which alone guarantees man his freedom. Authenticity demands that man stand alone, but with others, that he stand for himself, but also for others, in the process of making those choices which will affect all of life. His freedom to make these choices bespeak a respect arising out of responsibility toward the self and his fellowmen. Here is what Marcel is talking about in his concern that *everyman* be concerned about the *essential* dignity of man. Only the authentic person will treat one's fellowmen as another self, as a person equal to oneself and entitled to the same freedom. Could this ever be accomplished, asks Jaspers, without constant communication between the self and one's fellowman?

What is the relationship between existence and essence?

To repeat the question of Jaspers is to ask another: is there a dependency factor between existence and essence?

The existential mind could not function if this dependency factor did not exist. Does existence preceed essence is a question asked by every existentialist. However, to ask it suggests a paradox. Existence is the fact of *is;* it is *being.* Essence is what *being is.* Can the one exist, then, without the other; can one precede the other? To think so is nonsense.

To ask about the dependency factor between essence and existence is to ask about the totality of a man. A man is an involvement of the self with all confrontations in life. Man *is what he is* and *what he does* with the determinates in his life. Man is a total being and he reacts as a total being because of what he is and believes he can become. The existential mind is always asking: what are the basic conditions of *humanness?* How can man find meaning within these conditions? Man *is;* therefore, he exists; because he exists, he is something (essence); out of this something he makes of himself *more* than something. This requires a communication with the self; without it, he will never come to an understanding of his own potentiality.

Sartre's proposition: existence precedes essence, is meaningless. Man is always something. He is something because he is able to think; as a thinker, he is a pilgrim in search of knowledge and purpose. He believes that his world is understood as an external only as he internalizes its meaning for himself. He is in search of truth; here is something unique and applicable to only himself.

What is the real world? Man knows he can answer this only when he has validated his goals. And how does he validate goals? By knowing the meaning of truth. Truth is both infinite and finite; only in this way is truth its own subject matter; what it *is, is* what exists in its totality. The human mind has as its responsibility the apprehension of truth; truth is apprehended by degrees (the learning process) by means of the relevatory powers of its own being, namely, its subject matter. The real world, then, is an existent (this may be pluralized) apprehended by the mind by means of its experiential powers and actualized by the individual.

This 'subject matter' concept of existentialism is an intriguing one. It is like a two-way street; learning takes place when the revelatory powers of subject matter and the cognitive powers of the mind meet.

It is a matter of revelation and discovery. What 'happens' under the guidance of the teacher develops into the potentiality of apprehension and meaning for the learner. It is at this point in the learning process that creativity takes over. Truth evolves from the response of the mind; the search for truth must be within the guide posts provided by the spirit of truth. To be aware of the potentiality of this 'kind' of association is the first directive posited by existentialism. Here is a relationship which must be based on a need by the individual to identify the self with what *is* to be learned. Only in this way is the learner able to bring something to the learning process to the same degree that truth *brings* its subject matter.

What is the meaning of existentialism for education?

Here is the most important question for existentialism because its basic premises depend upon an applicative value to the learning process.

Values are not taught, nor can they be legislated. Values evolve from a mind stance; they imply the existence of goals and the recognition of the relevancy of conditions governing the attainment of those goals. Basic to this process is the ability of the learner to determine the validity of the 'ideas' which crowd him; to determine the potentiality of an idea by understanding all of its ramifications and implications is the educational goal of the existentialist. When the learner has attained this degree of intellectual sophistication, he has become an educable individual.

To think with an inquiring mind is to base this process on the premise that ideas learn from ideas. The methodology underlying this function of the process is the subject of the last two chapters of this book.

It is a matter of learning how to think *meaningfully*. Every thought must be looked upon as an intellectual frontier, as a source of new confrontations. Every idea must be seen and studied for its relevancy for the development of the self, to penetrate its shell of superficiality and permit the individual to become fully aware of his own potentialities by experiencing the *power* of meaning. He is dependent upon the idea to achieve this. *What happens by means of the idea is the responsibility of the teacher.* To pursue an idea is the starting point, an intellectual pilgrimage which can bring meaning to an individual. To learn with the student by experiencing a common perspective of awareness of inherent potentialities of an idea is to apprehend the meaningfulness of a relationship which holds value to be the embodiment of truth. It is upon this working premise the creative teacher is able to realize his own potentiality.

3

Creative Experience

Basic to self-understanding is the working premise of the creative teacher: to develop a philosophy of education is to increase one's understanding of the nature and destiny of man.

Even for the creative teacher, the word *philosophy* is a nebulous one; it is elusive in its nature, scope and purpose. Because of its complete dependency upon presuppositions, it means more than the search for wisdom. Philosophy is more than a scientific discipline or one of the arts of learning. *It is the learning process.* It is something more than a methodology; its essence is a spiritual hypothesis; it operates by means of a value condition and ultimately realizes itself in a value judgment. This is to say that it moves from one level of belief to another level of belief. The basic assumption here is that man lives, moves and has his being on some plane of judgment. The way he thinks and acts is done for some reason. When he acts or thinks differently he does so because he has changed levels of belief. This is the learning process or what is preferably called by the creative teacher, the development of a philosophy of learning.

The word *education* is even more elusive in its connotation. Teachers have often equated education with learning. This is a mistake. In most instances, and in a general sense, education is no more than a mechanical reaction to stimuli. It is a response of human sense to what is apparent. Learning far transcends the limitations of education.

It is the creative teacher who analyzes the methodology of the learning process and thus becomes aware of the basic tenets of an educational philosophy, cognizant of all facets of its functionary, the learning process.

— 1 —

The creative teacher is one who has carefully defined the concept of experience.

The creative teacher does not want to find himself in the same dilemma as Descartes, a philosopher so concerned with experience and its unrealities that he was unable to prove his own existence. The question of existence does not disturb the creative teacher; existence is an assumption of the hypothesis in the learning process. A person exists and, as an existent, it is necessary for him to learn in order to actualize himself.

The creative teacher realizes that the concept *experience* defies definition until its assumptions have been listed. These are:

Experience is a process. As a process, it is continuous and cumulative, internalizing its relationships. This is what makes it a concept and not a sensation. Sensations react to situations and are limited to their awareness of an environment; such awareness is based only on observation and not on the accumulation of knowledge and insight. Process infers a past; what has happened influences the experiential moment as well as subsequent experiences.

Experience actualizes itself in terms of an ultimate. As learning implies understanding, experience infers a deeper perception of the implications inherent in the material of knowledge, its principles and first cause. An understanding of ultimates is gained not from causes which are mere proximations, but from first principles.

Experience is subjective and objective in nature. Since experience deals in relationships, it is not concerned with the limitations normally imposed on subjectivity and objectivity. Relationships exist because of the interactivity which takes place in any cooperative process. Yet, it is not enough to say that experience is the interaction of an individual with his environment. Any process of interaction which is experienced by the mind culminates in the development of ideas and the ability to perceive the purely abstract. Experience requires an interplay between perception and thought.

The mind of experience expresses itself by means of its apprehension of projected ideas. This is to say, experiential value is realized as the mind reacts to yet another dimension of knowledge. The validity of perception depends upon the recognition and understanding of two distinct ideas. The learner may understand the inherent implications of the distinctive qualities of the ideas, but he experiences them as he apprehends their dependent relationships. Experience enables the learner to move from the level of possessing information to the plane of a cognitive totality which presupposes the existence of a conceptual learning scheme based on a logical sequence of ideas. Because the mind is here fully conscious of previously acquired concepts, experience is actualized when there is a synthesis of perceptions and the formulation of new concepts.

Experience does not objectivize; it is a process of interaction. To experience means to act by the means of its spiritual hypotheses; the mode of action is dependent upon the ideational perspective.

Experience actualizes the particular within the setting of the universal. All knowledge and its material bespeaks of logic which transcend sense experience; perception is dependent upon intellection concerned with a commonality of elements; sense knowledge alone is unable to perceptualize universals; to determine relationships among common elements is to form a concept of the universal by means of experiencing rational knowledge.

Experience provides a setting in which the learner is affected by his environment but realizes this is but one side of the coin of the concept. True experience is an activator; it is primarily interested in developing powers within the learner so he can transcend his environment and control it. As a power, experience is a dynamic process, disregarding the static and projecting new potentialities by means of a deeper understanding between particulars and universals. The mind experiences the whole through the relationships inherent in parts.

Experience is more than a cause and effect relationship. Experience means living within the consciousness of the implications of this relationship to the degree that thought reacts to an event and is thereby enabled to direct its influence and impact upon the powers of awareness in the learner. The mind of experience is intentional in nature. Because it has purpose, its perspective is to actualize meaning. There is no such thing as a 'random' experience within experience.

Experience is always conscious of its own potential. To experience an idea is to perceive its relations to other ideas as well as its value as an expansion-force in the consciousness of the learner.

Experience is largely phenomenological in character; its test in the learning process is the ability to intellectualize concepts. To experience is to think; it is to actualize the thought process in terms of the value it realizes. As a phenomenological event it concerns itself with the procedure of the thought process. At this point the learner becomes a phenomenologist because he considers experience as an event influencing his powers of judgment. Here is an example of the experiential process.

– 2 –

The creative teacher realizes that the primary responsibility of experience is the actualization of ideas.

The experiential mind possesses an abstractive power, the concern of which is the formulation of concepts. Experience is the reaction of its mind to the discoveries of the senses. By means of the energy inherent in a concept, relationships are determined and the ideas evolving through the process of thought subject the senses to an analysis of definitions for the purpose of establishing the validity of meaning.

An experience then, is the interaction between the learner's mind and the object of learning; it is the ability of the learner to react to the implicative directives of the concept evolving from the relationships between mind and its object in order to realize its meaning. Experiential value is value actualized by the mind rather than by the senses.

– 3 –

The creative teacher suggests there is a dichotomy in the statement: "there are many types of experience such as the educative and miseducative." The creative teacher believes no such distinction can be made.

Dewey, of course, thought otherwise. In this connection he was concerned with certain criteria, namely, continuity and interaction. He suggested that at the moment of experience, there is a basic *agreeableness*. This is what he meant by continuity. This agreeableness arouses curiousity, strengthens desire and sets up initiative to "carry a person over the dead places in the future." Furthermore, every experience bespeaks a kind of situation. Each situation comprises two types of experience, the objective and the internal. This is interaction because an experience is a transaction which takes place between the individual and his environment. To emphasize but one of these factors is mis-education.

Knowledge is derived from each experience, says the creative teacher, thereby making it an important factor in the learning process. Experience is educative whether it is identified with the everyday garden-type variety, which the learner simply accumulates, or is the result of systematic observation of the so-called practical aspects of life or their mediums of control. Nor does it mean that since a *practical* experience is *obtained* by work on the grass-roots level of learning it is of most value. All experience is both *controlled* and *practical* whether it is in the classroom or among a multitude of life's confrontations. Nor does it imply that the greatest *amount* of learning takes place by means of indirect experience. A basic premise in the concept of experience is an awareness arising from a consciousness of the relationship existing between a fact or an event and the human thought process. The question of origination and knowledge supplies its own answer when it is understood that knowledge evolves from experience. Such recognition will not support the contention that some experiences result from direct encounters and others from indirect confrontations. All knowledge is acquired through *direct* experience. This does not rule out the importance that because of the learning experience of others, a great deal of knowledge cannot come from them. Such knowledge must still be experienced by each learner. For instance, while the experience of Einstein enabled other scientists to invent the atomic bomb, each scientist had to experience the experience of Einstein before such knowledge could become meaningful. Direct experience is an individual matter and must be so tested. Since it is not distinct from rational knowledge, it is, nevertheless, the basis of every cognitive demand. Each experience gathers together its discoveries, whether general or universal, and posits them as hypotheses for further empirical study. Here is an inherent methodology which provides direction within the thought process. Thus, the creative teacher believes that experience is always more than a norm and endeavors to rise above the potential of the observable fact of an event. Experience is primarily an affair in knowing, a process which has as its perspective a knowledgeable action as well as an applicable result. Aristotle was correct when he stressed the need for continuity between thought and experience. While this seemingly differs from the position of the strict empiricist there is no harsh discontinuity between the two conditions. If the creative teacher holds to levels of experience, as in the case of Aristotle, his concern would soon be evident. In the process of knowledge is it possible to speak in terms of higher or lower levels? If so, it would have to be in terms of meaning as suggested by the linguistic analyst. While it is true that latitude in interpretation can convey different meanings to a fact or event, such freedom is limited by an inherent grammatical form. This situation alerts the learner to *degrees* of knowledge rather than to levels of experience. A declarative statement of fact is meaningful to the learner only when he is able to see meaning in its relationships. Experience stems from reflective thought, the act of perception. Experience is actual participation in the learning process.

— 4 —

The creative teacher believes that experience is both motivated by and motivates behavior.

Such behavior is fully conscious of inherent directives. In the learning process the mind is continually weighing evidence and deciding upon open avenues of action in order to realize meanings. Since experience is always a matter of conscious action it is purposive and does not fully react until aware of delineating factors. While there are degrees of knowledge, the only level of experience is awareness. Dewey is careful to point out that every experience is a moving force; it is *one with* inherent directives. Experience is the sole basis for experience.

— 5 —

The creative teacher, when he is confronted with the responsibility of defining experience is aware of the reality of the whole question of habit.

The concept of habit, for the creative teacher, is one accepted for what it is, something more than a mechanical response to a stimulus.

There are a number of conditions attached to the relationships engendered in any experience and all of them involve habit. Dewey understood this; for this reason he attached the presupposition *principle* to habit and suggested that it covers the formation of intellectual and emotional attitudes.

Experience is the kind of thing which is dependent upon the conditions, not mechanical but attitudinal. We react to the conditions and situations which constitute the construct of experience. Experience conditions and is conditioned by experience; therefore, this is why we may say that learning is a continuous process with one level of activity. Such a habit or conditions permits development in learning or, in reality, the experience of awareness.

The concept of essence was mentioned above. It was suggested that every attitude signifies the presence of an experience in process of realization. To determine the validity of an experience is to ascertain its essence. Essence is dependent upon definite aims.

To understand this proposition we again refer to Dewey's assumption that all learning relies heavily upon atmosphere. We know he depends upon individual responsibility to the point of the "self-construct" which bespeaks a recognition of the need for internal directives. The child, in order to be aware of the conditions of learning must experience the learning atmosphere or the essence of the thing being learned.

The idealist's concept of essence is always concerned with ultimates but only in reference to their responsibility to the immediate. What exists does so because it has essence and is, therefore, an ultimate. It is an ultimate because it exists at the moment and for the moment. In one sense, this tends to destroy the differential base of existence projected by the naturalists, pragmatists and perhaps even the realist. To be aware of an existent is to be able to realize its essence and therefore its meaning. To realize meaning is to imply the presence of a methodological process of interpretation.

— 6 —

The creative teacher believes that experience is valuable as a method because it helps to identify and estimate the potential of the developing factors inherent in the true learning process.

This means recognizing what comes first on the scale of dependency.

Experience makes way for further experience; we always move from the known through the unknown to the known. This is the learning process; logical thought is one characteristic of experience; this connotes the presence of a methodology which is rational in nature, scope and purpose. To experience, we move by means of the reasoning process, motivated by the presuppositions projected, to an understanding of the implications involved in an idea. It is the need to experience what we learn which gives value to what has been learned. All learning begins with the idea; to be aware of the practicality of the idea is to experience its potentiality. This is the meaning of *instrumentalism.*

All this implies that we have gone further than the realists and the rational humanists even though the latter will go as far as natural reason and metaphysics seemingly will permit them to go. Method in experience suggests that we look for deeper meaning in meaning. This does not suggest an unfaithfulness to the empirical method; true empiricism looks for a type of experiential value which connotes purpose realized in everything which is learned. What method is after, then, in the learning process is to open subject matter to the point of determining its relationships by destroying the concept that each fact is an entity.

Experience realizes itself through the spiritual connectives provided by a rational methodology. This suggests that each new experience is actualized only when preceeding experiences have been realized as being meaningful.

We learn as we experience; knowledge is the resultant of experience. This is the empirical view of the learning process; but while we attach the *a posteriori* label to it, it often becomes difficult to distinguish this from the so-called *a priori* tag which says that knowledge is gained by reason alone and not through experience itself. Of course there are empiricists who admit *a priori* knowledge and its dependency, but only in relation to mathematics and logic. Locke, for instance, was adamant in his belief that all knowledge comes through the senses; sensation and reflection providing the mind with its raw materials. These two factors, then, serve as the two sources for the idea. Another example would be certain facets of pragmatism which stresses that experience is the best test for the validity of beliefs.

While we say that epistemology is the study of the nature of knowledge, it confronts us with the demand for methodology based on the question: "How does the learner know?" This raises such other questions as: "What is knowledge?" and "How does the learner internalize the external world?" All of this suggests another dimension in methodology, namely, perception.

Kant held that we perceive through our senses but the *what* of perception is the important thing. His concern was with the ability of the mind to order its own experience. Not all knowledge is experienced, but the experience aspect comes into play when the mind coordinates the sensations into ideas and further molds the plurality of thought into some semblance of order and continuity. While it is true that all this attests to *a priori* knowledge, its rational base guarantees us a wider connotative value for experience. The best example of this is found in Aristotle's position. Aristotle believed that experience was an important ingredient of the *real* world, the real world being the natural world in the process of change.

Many philosophers have tried to reconcile the apparent differences between permanence and change in reality. It will be recalled that Plato perceived the real world as the world of ideas and the sense world only became real when it affected or was affected by the realm of ideas. Here, too, he was touching upon this new ingredient in experience. For it is something more than the traditional argument between appearance and reality. Is it possible that some system exists which is able to explain the structure of reality outside of its relationship to a given discipline? Science is never a system *of* something; rather, it is a *knowledge* of the parts of a whole which is greater than the sum of those same parts. This is what is meant by metaphysics.

Philosophers also disagree about the definition of metaphysics. Almost all agree, however, that it is concerned with the implicative interpretation of experience. This means a concern for the potentiality of *what* exists; to determine purpose in potentiality there must be the presence of a methodology which will permit clear and consistent thinking. This was the position of William James. Kant likewise held that metaphysics is transcendent, concerned only with what is possible. On this basis we could say that reality (in this sense, experience) is founded on both change and permanence. This was taught by Aristotle when he said that experience is the important path in the development of the learner's conscious life. Experience here is equated with reality and the one thing which gives meaning to both *becoming* and *being*. Aristotle believed that life is a process of becoming and both change and permanence are an integral part of existence.

What we have been talking about here is perceptual experience; we must think in terms of an *order* in reality. To understand an *order* the learner must base his approach on a methodology unified by a relevancy principle. Such unification takes place within the mind alone. Like Hume, we believe that the mind is an abstract name for a series of ideas. By means of perception we are enabled to know the mind in the same way as we know the material of knowledge. The mind is built upon every facet of the process of experience. Thus, we are projecting Whitehead's dictum that experience is basic to understanding and necessary in the promotion of man's potentiality. Knowledge is gained by means of the establishment of a matrix, therefore, a methodology. This far transcends Berkeley's stand on matter only as form of the mind. Knowledge is more than its contingent sensations.

Experience is aware of the implications of change and the relevancy of the permanent. Experience is always expectant of more experience. The factor which keeps this expectation alive is perception.

— 7 —

Perception, for the creative teacher, is one of the most active and powerful forces in the learning process. It is never passive and means much more than merely receiving impressions from an external world.

In and by means of perception, the learner *re-constitutes* the relational process inherent in understanding the *fact*. Reflective thought and reason is an integral part of the learning process. To perceive is to discover, understand and become aware of the unity inherent in the material of knowledge. It means finding sequence in the existent and discovering the logic in each construct.

— 8 —

The idea, for the creative teacher, is one of the keys to an understanding of experience.

The idea originates in and by means of experience; it is spontaneously generated. It has been stated above that experience is the result of an interaction between the mind of the learner and all facets of his environment; the learner finds meaning in what he is learning as he experiences it. The *idea* evolves out of each experience and serves as a working hypothesis between mind and the object of learning. This is reflective thought.

The learner who is learning because he is experiencing understands that he is involved in a creative process. The true learner is always a free functioning individual who is *becoming* as he realizes the potential inherent in each new experience. Such a person is *becoming* because he is open to the implications inherent in each experience. This is the reason for suggesting that an idea, if it serves its true purpose as a working hypothesis is open-ended. Only this *kind* of idea can become creative.

A working hypothesis is a theory which has as its concern the realization of relationships and principles inherent in existing phenomena. Its perspective is the formulation of purpose; without the realization of purpose, experience is without a goal, namely, to test what *is*. To experience is to understand that facts alone do not constitute knowledge. While each fact has an individual character it is wholly dependent upon other facts to give it meaning. This requires the use of the hypothesis in order to organize a pattern of facts (which may structure the core of knowledge). Observation of data must lead (in order to be meaningful) into an understanding of a structure which becomes a working hypothesis upon which to act and react. It is at this point that experience serves as a test of the hypothesis. Experience draws on previous experience and knowledge. Experience is built upon the premise that values perceived in one setting may well serve as the working base in another experience. Experience makes use of these values and ultimately they become the material of knowledge.

Experience, then, has one objective, to aid the learner to think effectively. To think means the learner has mastered the art and science of analysis, criticism and evaluation. In other words, he has developed a methodology which possesses many of the characteristics of the scientific method. Since one of the premises of this theory of experience is the need to provide meaning through an awareness of implicative purpose, Dewey's insistence not only upon observation and judgment as integral factors in this process, but his emphasis on significance becomes readily apparent. To be aware of significance is, in his words, to select (be able to) the kind of present experiences that live fruitfully and creatively in subsequent experiences. Dewey defines education as the reconstruction or reorganization of experience, and which increases ability to direct the course of subsequent experiences.

Experience is an important means of control when the subject of *consequence* is taken into consideration. Intention by means of control is an important concept in the philosophy of education. To intend is to anticipate; here is the working hypothesis. The creative teacher is aware of the need to ready the learner to realize the most beneficial consequences of the learning process. In a sense, then, the creative teacher controls the learning experience. He controls the condition of experience so that what is learned in an experience determines its applicative value. To do this, there must be interaction between the learner and the learned. Experience must become so sophisticated that it knows how to prepare the learner for future experiences. However, such interaction is more than the confrontation of subject by an object. It is the resolution of experiential problems and the transformation of an indeterminate problematic situation into one which is coherent and determinate in the many meanings it contains. This, in essence, is Dewey's position.

The object of learning is realized when it becomes meaningful; that is, when the learner sees its relevancy to some reasoned need. The learning process as the art and science of experiencing implies an interaction between the *how* and *what* of thinking. To find meaning in a fact and its relationships is to have experienced and solved it.

The student of the philosophy of education is familiar with Dewey's position that experience enables the individual to reach wider and deeper unifications of the self with the material of knowledge or matter. To this the creative teacher would add: in this process it is the totality of the individual and his environment which is involved in the experiencing situation. Peculiar to the individual is a unique ability to develop a life organization or dynamic life pattern.

Such interaction with others gives the individual his learning stance. This is to say that experience is individual and personal in definition. Thought and its processes is always on an individual basis; each learner possesses his own field of learning association. Therefore, an experience should be the perception and integration of the totality of awareness of an object of learning at a given moment and in a given circumstance.

Experience is concerned with the process of change as it affects the behavior of the learner within the totality of the self. The need for change, in any setting, presupposes a confrontation between the self and a problem. This is a working premise for experience; experience endeavors to make it possible for the learner to achieve self understanding. To do so, the learner must realize that only 'he' can experience the object of learning and do so existentially. The learner can never separate himself from the experience of learning. Only in this way does he come to terms with the material of knowledge. Experience originates in, is a part of, and has its fulfillment in this confrontation. It is the process of interaction between the learner and the learning problem. This implies that a synthesis has been reached within the learner's cognitive framework, and he has become sensitive to the emergent meanings which he encounters within himself. Pure knowledge should have no meaning for the learner. This is also true when he is confronted with the mere existence of the *object* of learning. Experience demands interaction in this setting in order to understand and further reflect upon meaning and application. Experience demands that all complications be defined and related in a significant way to value conditions. An experience is meaningful only as it is identified by and related to the learner. Dewey emphasized the need for the learner to be given access to experiences which will enrich his life and possibly make him a better person. This suggests a basic freedom to experience what others have experienced. His concern was with the atmosphere of freedom as an integral part of the essence of experience. Dewey in this respect was close to the philosopher Kierkegaard who maintained that the only freedom of importance is the freedom to think. Dewey's position implies that the only freedom of enduring importance is the freedom of intelligence. The learner must have the freedom to achieve within the limits of his capacity. It is the teacher's responsibility to initiate the material of knowledge that will enable activities to be selected which lend themselves to synthesis and interpretation.

True learning as a natural process is the result of integrating experiences. Perhaps this is contrary to Descartes's position that experience has no role in the growth of knowledge within the individual. Instead, the individual is born with innate ideas which ultimately are expressed or revealed by means of divine guidance. Seemingly, the material of knowledge pivots on the axis of a revelation of truth.

On the other hand, the realist in contrast with the idealist looks upon experience as a tool for learning, as a means of analyzing and interpretating experiences, almost to the point of forcing the individual to think and make decisions.

If we hold to the premise that experience is what happens *to* as well as happens *by* an individual, we would, by necessity, have to strongly disagree with Descartes and many of the idealists. Even the realist is weak in his interpretation at this point. To limit experience as a tool is to destroy its true responsibility.

To experience is to actualize the object of learning. This is what Kilpatrick meant when he said that learning is inherent in experience itself. When the learner brings to a close each stage of experience with an acceptable solution, such experience continues to influence later stages. This factor gives unity and coherence to later experiences and to life itself. The foundation for the next step is determined when it was accepted by and acted upon by the individual.

Experience characterizes the learning process as a laboratory in which the learner destroys subject matter lines of limitation and emphasizes units. The learner uses questions and ideas to shape the curriculum in such a way as to experience the material of knowledge by means of the development of new ideas. The teacher is looked upon here as a guide enabling the learner to actualize his learning potential.

The quality of experience, therefore, the quality of knowledge, acquired by the learner is of the utmost importance. And this goes far beyond the limitations of whether what is learned is agreeable or disagreeable to the learner. While an experience may not always be looked upon as good, if it is an experience, it is meaningful. Every experience has a qualitative factor inherent in its being; an experience is never static; it always endeavors to stimulate. A learning stimulant is concerned with both quality and the consistency which undergirds continuity. Its primary responsibility is not the development of interest. This factor is taken care of under the concept of motivation.

The quality of an experience is dependent upon the nature of the reaction in the learning process. Such reactions are qualitative in meaning, those which guide the learner toward the satisfaction gained from the acquisition, assimilation and application of knowledge. It was Locke who said that all our knowledge comes from experience and through our senses. His working premise was: there is nothing in the mind except what is first in the senses.

The creative teacher believes, then, that the learner's most unique function is the power of his intelligence. Regardless of the position of a particular philosopher, the working premise is always the mind. Kant tried to prove that knowledge does not come by sense experience but through pure reason. What else is this but the responsibility of the mind? Hobbes and Berkeley side with Locke when they say that experience is the only source of knowledge. This is the pure empirical position; the existence of the abstract or the universal in the formulation of the mind is rejected. Aristotle emphasized the role of experience in arriving at first principles or what was called real knowledge. Here knowledge of universals is sought, while for the empiricist, experience calls for the accumulation of facts. For Dewey it was: ". . . .so act as to increase the meaning of present experience." For many reasons, Whitehead and Russell are of the same mind. Whitehead held that knowledge is conscious discrimination of objects experienced. Knowledge for Russell is experience in science which enables the learner to predict the acquisition of knowledge. The knowledge experienced, according to Whitehead, is a product of deliberate conscious activity. Each of these philosophers, in essence, is saying the same thing. The power of intelligence is the learner's most unique function, and it resides in his mind. Every experience, because of its qualitative value, conditions the learner to better realize the meaning of relationships.

To live critically and responsibly should be the aim of every learner; to achieve this aim is the function of the school; it must recognize the impact of the experiential process. This involves the responsibility of living intelligently and finding meaning in a trenchant social experience. Learning takes place by means of the active utilization and realization of such experience.

Experience is the inner eye of the learner. To develop the sense of awareness required by experience in order to realize itself is the chief responsibility of the creative teacher; he is fully aware of the limitations of repetition, drill and memorization in the learning process. He also knows there must be stronger factors at work such as reflective thought stimulating an active, persistent inquiry, and the examination and evaluation of the material of knowledge. This means that the creative teacher's part in the task of learning is more than furnishing the environment which stimulates responses and directs the course of the learner. The creative teacher will do more than modify the stimuli so that response will (or should) result in the formation of an intellectual reaction.

Learning takes place in the presence of a problem which the creative teacher will relate to an experiential process which is within the range and potentiality of the student. The creative teacher knows that if the material of knowledge is to have meaning it will have to be related to an essential problem in which the learner has the interest to clarify and resolve. To teach in such a way that the student experiences the material of knowledge and becomes aware of the importance of the implicative value of a certain subject or object for him personally is to realize meaning in the art and science of being a catalyst in the learning process.

– 9 –

The creative teacher believes that inquiry is an integral part of the learning process.

Inquiry implies the freedom to think and to do so without the restraints of presuppositions or predetermined procedures while at the same time finding it necessary to discipline itself to a critical process of analysis. This is not a contradiction in perspective for the emphasis is one of systematic methodology. This process is characteristic of the inquiring mind.

The inquiring mind can be analyzed as to its nature by listing facets of its critical attitude toward theory, philosophy and truth.

Theory

Knowledge and truth are not always synonymous in essence; truth is the goal towards which the learner strives by means of the perspectives furnished by knowledge. To get the best hold on truth is the learner's aim; in the process of accomplishing this, he should be aware of the need to exert judgment as he appraises ideas.

While theory may be invented by the human mind, the learner is cognizant of the need to verify a theory; this is done when facts explain theory. Facts permit the learner to experience the idea in a more concrete way. Truth is something more than an idea and connotes the realization of what otherwise may have remained but a point in the realm of the abstract. While truth evolves from the idea, it corresponds to fact and literally coheres with the knowledge attained.

Because the mind is concerned first with the theory which evolves from the idea, its basic demand for consistency and coherence is met.

The mind cannot justify its methodology if the above need is not met; only then can an idea be studied against the available related knowledge and compared to determine consistency. Truth is the full materialization of fact, either particular or general; it is both comprehensive and consistent. It is coherence which enables the learner to experience truth; there is the complete harmonization with knowledge. For the human mind, there are degrees in the apprehension of truth.

A theory is a proposition; as such, it seeks to determine relationships between ideas. This relationship implies more than agreeableness and consistency between ideas. Theory studies the fabric of what is known; but what is known presupposes limitation. Theory comes into its own when it endeavors to move beyond apparent limitations; its task is to unite the idea with reality. Truth exists even without the learner's knowledge of it; it *exists* for the learner *when* he experiences it.

Because truth is First Cause and its nature exudes theory and idea, it infers the need for a highly rational series of hypotheses and conclusions empirically verified. As a part of this process, one of its tests for realization is coherence.

Philosophy

The inquiring mind is philosophically oriented. This is necessary if the mind is to determine the implications of the working principles which structure the body of truth. The philosophical mind is aware of the unity and coherence which comprises the realm of truth. To apply these principles to the particulars of a created universe is something which only the philosophical mind can do. The universe is a living organism, and, can be understood only against the recognition of this tenet.

Truth is never imposed upon the human mind; to be realized and experienced, it must be actualized by the learner. Truth is characterized by its wholeness; to attain such apprehension is to know that learning is a process of step by step confirmation of what is discovered as an organism. Inherent in every organism is a unity and integrity. To find the principles which have brought the unity and integrity into being is to find truth.

The philosophical mind does not permit parts to be abstracted from the whole; to its way of thinking, an entity does not exist. The whole (truth) functions according to laws (principles) and parts are knowable only in relation to the complete organism. This is the working principle of coherence.

Truth

Truth is experienced as it evolves from the process of learning. This is an activity of the mind as it understands the implications of an orderly wholeness which makes itself intelligible through its principles of revelation. Truth is apprehended when thought and reality agree and integrate.

Truth is never relative; it is the apprehension of truth by the learner which is relative. This does not affect the ordered wholeness of truth; rather, it bespeaks of judgment as the apprehension of the degree of truth or falsity, and resides in the learner's knowledge of truth, in the inquiring mind.

— 10 —

The creative teacher is aware that coherence is a depth concept, which means that the learner, in order to understand must experience meaning as truth by realizing its wholeness through its dependency upon continuity and consistency.

To suggest that coherence implies a sticking-together process only is to abuse its importance as a principle of learning. While it has been stated that with coherence the learner sees the whole, this is not to avoid the atomistic method. Rather, it is to propound the belief that truth possesses an inner core from which emanates a perspective depicting the design described by consistency and continuity. Parts are seen in relation to the whole and the whole as dependent upon the relation of its parts. This is the internal perspective which the existent seeks to make available to the learner as he compiles his knowledge of the parts in order to reconstruct the whole.

To do this, ideas are all-important. Ideas are developmental in nature and become meaningful only when they are seen in relation to one another. Ideas depend upon one another just as facts carry implications for all other facts; each fact exists because it is a part of a harmonious system.

It will be recalled that Plato looked upon learning as a process and the mind as something capable of intellectualizing the principles of truth. For him, the mind was not a storage plant. His concern was with ideas and their freedom to develop. A true idea cannot stand in contradiction to another idea; with the absence of coherence there is the presence of falsity. Since truth is rational, the ideas concerning it must be rational in order for knowledge to permit its apprehension. This is achieved when there is agreement between facts and their relations, laws of objectivity, and judgments of the inquiring mind. It is the mind which brings to this process the demand for consistency and continuity in theory and in idea.

Relationships emphasize direction; this is a necessary ingredient in the learning process. Relationships imply both internal and external consistency; such congruency demands of the material of knowledge (because of its rational nature) that its basic attribute remain unchangeable when its relation to other materials change. There is an ultimate unity in all material of knowledge. Basic nature, or the universal, while often contingent on its relationship to particulars, is never changed, while relationships among facts or particulars may often change. Thus, relationships are internal as well as external and the direction for their development is found inside the process of determining the degree of cohesiveness necessary to guarantee continuity.

Coherence, then, is a depth concept, implying that the learner, in order to *understand* must experience meaning as truth by realizing its wholeness through its dependency upon continuity and consistency. Facts are but one means of learning truth; in order to be meaningful they must conform to the *being* of reality which has as its task the synthesis of the material of knowledge into an ordered whole.

As ideas depend upon other ideas for their development, experience as an activity underlying the learning process exists for the sake of begetting other experience. Learning takes place when one experience leads to another experience and the meaning between the two brings into being the insight necessary for comprehension. With unification of thought, ideas are then given the opportunity to qualify their position with respect to other ideas and develop their necessary sequential patterns.

To qualify their position with respect to responsibility in the learning process and achieve the sequence necessary for the actualization of meaning, each idea and all facets of experience recognize that the structural principle of logic can exist only within a logical and rational system of thought; logic has the responsibility of explaining what already exists as a rational design.

As a science, because of its methodology, logic has been classified in many ways, but primarily as the Aristotelian route of deduction, and the later path laid out by the inductive philosophers such as Bacon and John Stuart Mill. It has been the latter which has served so well in the development of modern science and has now come to be known as formal logic. However, regardless of the classification or emphasis, logic continues to be recognized as a methodological instrument assuring efficiency of thought. Logical reasoning is its goal and its concern is with the principles of valid argument. To accomplish this, its precepts pertain to the definition, classification and use of terms and the ideas behind them, the appraisal of the significance of concepts, and the place of inference in the scale of valuation, all of which are ultimately concerned with the problem of coherence in the learning process.

The logician is an epistemologist concerned with the process of reasoning. He is introspective, by nature; his task is to develop and internalize the learning perspective. He knows that only in this way will he find the principles which undergird coherence and the nature of the material of knowledge. Only as he masters this internal technique will he be enabled to validate knowledge and the methods for determining its foundations and limitations.

In the development of a philosophy of education the demand of logic and coherence when met, will assure an agreement of thought in relation to the real responsibility of the learning process, namely, to find meaning in ideas and concepts. Truth is a matter of relationships, the spirit which exists between two minds, both of which constitute reality.

The concept of coherence and its responsibility to educational theory as well as the burden of learning process toward its directives as an integral part of the methodology of teaching, rests upon one assumption, namely, the creative teacher; because he understands how one learns, will never attempt to teach facts alone. A fact is meaningless if looked at as an entity. Learning, therefore understanding, takes place when a fact coheres with the material of knowledge already mastered; only then, is meaning found and realized. It was Whitehead who reminds the creative teacher that one of the most useless bores on God's earth is the merely well-informed man. To receive information is different from learning and appraising its implicative value.

Coherence is the salve of the learning process because its relevance is so meaningful to every facet of education. Its essence and significance implies more than the structuring of a system of knowledge in which its material for learning has been determined by the laws of logic; as Brubacher says, it is the integration of knowledge with experience and life itself. When we look closely at coherence we can see that its aim, when applied to the learning process is total self-realization. The creative teacher here serves as a source of inspiration and guidance, one unwilling to *tell* the learner *about* some facet of the material of knowledge, but rather enables him to learn by means of integrating the environment of education. This teacher believes that the learner must master his environment and never submit to it; his is the power of change and control; build and destroy if necessary, but most of all, reconstruct what needs to be changed. In this way, the learner grows, with consistency, in the *conditions* of environment. This is the way culture has come into being; it has been *created*.

It is consistency in a curriculum which permits the learner to venture into the realm of the abstract. It is this venture which humanizes the learning process by permitting the student to verify his thinking. Without such a journey, learning stagnates; it is coherence which brings about depth in what is learned. Depth in learning is reached when consistency and coherence literally *build up* a sequence of knowledge *totals* and thereby creates an integration of the mind from within. Coherence is insistent that learning is an internal process; it believes that the whole is greater than the sum of parts. Man is an integrated whole; and, he learns by developing order among his mental attitudes. As ideas learn from other ideas, attitudes are linked together cognitively; they are dependent upon one another for meaning. The learner soon finds it necessary to evaluate his presuppositions in light of experiencing new knowledge. To learn is to strengthen what one already knows as truth or untruth. This is done by testing and verification. Both of which, if their methodologies are correct, will reveal inconsistencies and disunity so that they may be changed to develop a philosophy of learning possessing the characteristic of coherence. This suggests that we revert back to our original premise: the most important function of the learning process is to realize knowledge and its material by using facts only in relation to other facts. The creative teacher has one responsibility: to enable the student to learn how to test facts in order to find what relational values they hold. Truth does not change; it is the learner's interpretation of his ability for perception of the truth which changes. It is this power of perception which tells him that facts are not complete in themselves. It is by means of the method of coherence within the learning process that he is enabled to find the relationship between fact and truth.

4

The Creative Teacher

The creative teacher believes that education is problematic and never static; thinking begins in the presence of a problem.

The teacher who is fully aware of the coherent demands in the learning process understands that his task is to experience the same fascination for the language of knowledge (words and the conveyance of ideas) as does the educative process in its relation to all the arts, but with the added responsibility of learning the methods and modes of interpreting the same words and ideas and relating these to particular needs and desires. Each word in the language of learning is designed in such a way that, given its proper place, will aid in the development of an idea. Ideas correctly constructed will unravel the learner's need. This is what gives sense to words and meaning to a learning perspective. Both the teacher and learner must scan the same coherent landscape.

Each word in the language of learning will have an effect upon the learner, and it must be construed in terms of ideas which are definitive in nature, wide in scope and inflective in purpose. The dimension of the language of learning finds its limitation in the impression which it leaves on the mind.

Impression and experience are the motivating factors in any type of activity. The functional purpose and aim of the learner must be to achieve this end, and his aptitude for learning will be determined by his ability to understand words and ideas and translate them into the language of impression and experience.

The ideal of learning includes a concern for *correct understanding*. Both words are necessary, the one connoting *method* and the other *content*.

To educate is to insure understanding through a persistent effort of coherent thought. Learning is a constant movement in the learner's persistent effort to acquire understanding. Understanding is the knowledge of all other things related to these principles and tenets; it is the knowledge of integration and coherence, the ability to recognize the dependency of subject matter on subject matter.

The limitation of study does not comprise the physical totality of the object; its measurements include more than the height, width and depth. The subject is dependent upon the material used, its plasticity, the ability of the learner and his perspective. All of this must be read as the object of learning *becomes* its own blueprint.

It is not given to any art or science to walk alone; no subject can stand apart.

Education is more than the possession of knowledge. Knowledge without understanding is lifeless. Education is the constant pursuit to understand what is coherent and vital in and to life. It is true that many educational philosophers have considered education to be life itself, that education is experiencing the wholeness of life.

It is the educator who has sensed the ideal of learning that carried with it the idea of conquering the obstacles of the mind and unifying understanding with life. In this instance, education is defined as nurture, the determining factor within the process of understanding used to direct and control life to move towards its highest and truest purpose. The creative teacher provides the direction; it is the content of the material of knowledge which will fulfill purpose.

To do this, the creative teacher senses the need of implementation in subject and content; education is movement by progression through a lifetime. To be educated means to be so through every experience of life. To prepare the learner for this demands a careful analysis of the purpose and method of learning by the teacher. In a sense, education demands more than any one teacher can give; but, to find and give direction will always remain his primary task. His second responsibility is to enable each student to become his own teacher. It is not enough for the creative teacher to *know* his subject and its content, nor, is it sufficient for him to tell the learner *what* to learn; this method offers no assurance of assimilation. Assimilation of subject matter (the material of knowledge) means there has been self-realization. In self-realization, the learner has grasped meaning.

One question always uppermost in the mind of the creative teacher is related to methodology. What is the best method or the proper way to teach? The teacher, at this point in his thinking, is not speculating about the method used in implementation of subject matter. Rather, he is searching for a method which he, as a person, feels is necessary to use in providing the learner with sufficient motivation to arouse interest and curiosity to the degree of desire to think deeply at the well of subject and content, and to provide the means whereby satisfaction may be gained through aggregation of subject, content and the possibilities of assimilation.

What does it do for the learner? It makes him aware of the entire field of which his subject is a part. He becomes aware of the work already completed on the subject through experiment and research, and what lies unfinished. The creative teacher is always aware that the tools of his profession, the discussion, lecture, textbook, have their place, and to some extent, implement knowledge. These methods of instruction *exercise the capacity of the intellect.* Knowledge *about* a subject can be acquired from the textbook or the lecture; patterns for experimentation can be taught through statement and discipline. Latin Europe's seven-fold classification of the liberal arts can be learned by way of the book or test tube. But it is an educational task only half completed.

Learning must be permitted to define itself. It is an ability for integrated coherent thought which makes the difference in the educational task. The answer is found in the learning process. The student may learn a great deal about chemistry, and not become a chemist. He may have the aptitude for learning a language, without becoming a linguist. He may be able to master the techniques of politics, but become only a politician instead of a statesman and diplomat. He may possess an analytical mind, teach mathematics, but never become a mathematician. Education tells us we may know a great deal about subject and content without actually falling heir to that creative experience which makes out of the mathematics instructor the mathematician.

Not to possess knowledge alone, then, is the goal of education, but rather, to master its language.

We may see it in the type of relationship which exists between the reader, the poem and the poet. The same questions are asked as when confronted with the problem of defining education by way of the creative relationship between the learner, the subject and content, and the teacher. The literateur asks: how, when, and why is a poem written? It would not be fair to say that every poem must answer, in itself, these questions. The same is true for the material of knowledge. Nevertheless, the poet (and the teacher) should be conscious of the question being asked. Seldom should a poem be read without these thoughts being firmly lodged in the mind of the reader. It is the touchstone of the creative experience. To say that a poem writes itself, is not enough. First, the process itself must be creative. This is the *something* which makes the poem as well as gives validity to the learning process. This something is what makes the historian instead of the instructor in history. It is what gives life to words and phrases and life to subject and content.

Closest of all educators to translating the science of learning into a philosophy of coherent language was Jan Amos Komensky (Comenius, 1592-1670). In his *The Analytical Didactic* he developed a philosophy of the coherent life. The object of learning and mastering the material of knowledge, he said, is to understand what is revealed *by* the world and the human mind. To learn is *by way* of motivation, aggregation and assimilation. Knowledge is universal in nature; it is a language which all men should be able to understand. Understanding is the erasure of friction in the learning process. The road to peace between man and men is an academic journey, passing through the city of Education, bypassing the rubble of human folly, namely, war. Education is nurture, in and for life. It is the recognition of what the mind of God *can* mean for the person willing to study it (the material of knowledge). God, he says, is Scripture, nature and mind. This faith was real for Comenius, not something apparent. It is the learning process as a way, not a system; it is Pansophy, the language of learning.

He saw education as a matter of relationships. As the soul is to the body, so is content to the subject, knowledge to the intellect, education to wisdom and the creative experience of learning to *use* the coherent language which the human mind is begging to develop.

Understanding the mechanics of education by way of learning to use its language is another method whereby the creative teacher regulates the development of the learning process as it becomes the subject of identification by the student. There is no learning without first understanding the learning process. One cannot understand subject or content unless insight is provided through the functional relationship which must exist between the learner and what he is learning. The learner must possess the ability to *create;* the patterns of education serve no other purpose than providing the spiritual incentive for *using* what has been learned. To create anew out of *how* and *what* he has learned is an important goal of every learner.

To *achieve* for its own sake is not the perspective of this goal. To search for, and *possess* truth, and then not know *how* or *when* to use it, is not a mark of the educated man. To *achieve* in order to *use* (to teach) is the highest goal for which we must strive in the academic realm. And to achieve what is coherent, consistent and logical is the direction in which this goal lies. But it is something more than direction; it is self-realization.

Education, without benefit of its language of learning, suggests a disorganized, illogical, inconsistent and incomprehensible whole. But education, with the benefit of its language, suggests (because there is self-realization in and a part of the mind of the learner) a universe governed by logic and reason. It is a universe which demonstrates organization and integration. Within the universe, there is an inter-relatedness of all things regardless of its state of development or decay.

The universe is no puzzle; it is a structured, spiritually-patterned, coherent whole.

Education demands of the mind the ability to perceive subject and content in their logical consistency as these ideas relate, through subject integration, to content. Thus the need for a well-balanced, well-integrated curriculum is apparent.

The curriculum, as one of the words in the language of education (as a conveyance used in the expression of ideas) is the most tangible of all tools at the command of the creative teacher. It should be the most plastic. It is the structure of the curriculum which must recognize the learner's need for growth and development and which not only teaches content, but the methods of assimilation as well. It is at this point the learner should see subject and content in the context of the language of education, its wholeness and application to need. To achieve this, the curriculum calls into play its spokesman, the creative teacher, who must travel together with the student in learning its language. Education is the marrow of life; it must live to be effective. Its language is not dead, but speaks plainly of the way.

Education has no existence outside its language. Philosophies of education come and go with men searching for its definition. Education subsists in itself, but for the life of the learner; it invites the learner to listen, to follow; it does not come ready-made and packaged. What it has to teach must be learned. It is both quest and conquest. Education leads the inquiring mind to its own source; it alone motivates the inquiring mind; it gives no gift, but is aids in the birth of an educationally oriented life; it is the experience of learning and language of achievement.

Education possesses a sacred duty, for it alone holds the key to method for the unification of all sources which constitute the spiritual oriented life.

Education, like learning, is a process, teaching the use of language found within the plasticity of subject and content for the transmission of words and ideas, and the values, the experience of actualization in growth and development by means of the awareness of what life makes possible to the learner.

— 1 —

The creative teacher believes that the learning process is an ideal, patterned by its attitude toward and dependency upon eight assumptions:

1. All learning implies understanding. The purpose of education is to understand man's source of motivation for learning the *how* and *why* of his drive to comprehend the relevatory powers of truth;

2. The key to scholarship lies within the mind's attitude toward learning. Scholarship is the product of mental activity; it depends upon the sense of direction provided by method and the sense of experimentation programmed by the mind. Thus the *whole* of learning is created, brought into being and seen as a product of the creative mind when two or more proved facts unite and give birth to a new life, a new fact;

3. Knowledge, though it varies according to individual intelligence, experience and maturity, through its nature reveals a methodology for the unfolding of its material to the human mind;

4. Intellection is a value condition of the learning process; it is this process which makes learning meaningful;

5. Bias is a bent intellection;

6. All value is contingent upon the purposive activity of the learner;

7. The question is dependent upon the learner's ability to develop ideas through his power to reason and his ability to search for the answer *why;*

8. Fragmentation destroys the integrative core in education, namely, what is universal in its nature.

The learning process is vitally concerned with the eight concepts inherent in the above assumptions. In fact, it is suggested that the process realizes itself only when the problems of learning, scholarship, knowledge, intellection, bias, the value condition, the question and fragmentation are met and answered.

One of the lost arts in education today is contemplation. It is practically non-existent in today's classroom. It is the contention of the creative teacher that he must teach for contemplation and this requires time and the open-ended idea.

An idea is open at both ends. This proposition provides the grist for contemplation.

It is a reaction common to teachers to wonder about results. What *was* accomplished in the fifty minutes of instruction? And, how does the teacher react to his own question? By testing himself against the test results of the students. Very often, because of his own insecurity and uneasiness in his teaching field and in order to salve the academic conscience, the test will be given while the material is still fresh. It seems to help the situation all the way around. Does it, really?

Educators should teach for contemplation. Not in order to make of students mystics, religious or secular, but to assist them to think philosophically, to teach them how to reflect. As they reflect, they will question, doubt, analyze, synthesize and design hypotheses. In other words, they will be actively engaged in the thought process, experiencing as they think. As they reflect they will envision alternatives, destroy boundaries and limitations and react to consequences. Only in reflection is the *significant* realized and understood. To reflect requires the opportunity to analyze the potential force inherent in every fact. Reflection is concerned with the kind of thinking which is logical in its methodology and consistent in its demand for the correct handling of *the concept*. For in the thought process it is possible to dissect the concept and determine its relevancy to learning. This is what is meant by contemplation. Contemplation takes us much deeper into the thought process. It is a kind of dialogue with the self, recognizing that in reflection alternative positions and solutions to a common problem will reside in an open mind. One does not reflect upon nothing; the human mind is filled with a knowledge which can be classified only as antecedent. To evaluate these, subjecting them to a theoretical operation, is to determine their relevancy in the learning process. To be able to do this means the student is thinking effectively; he is contemplating.

Attitudes are very important in the learning process. Attitudes reflect the kind of thinking that is taking place; they suggest that learning recognizes that its goal includes more than the accumulation of knowledge. The reflective attitude is based on principles which arise out of developing factors inherent in theory and *speculation on the fact*. By means of such an attitude the learner is able to gain a perspective of what the fact is saying and suggesting. Facts become meaningful only in relation to other facts. No fact stands or can remain in isolation. The reflective attitude demands that each fact is placed in its proper niche and studied together with other facts in a unified whole. To think reflectively is to be aware of the principles which govern the fact and its relations. This is as close as we can come to a meaning of transcendent thought attitude. Transcendent thought is concerned with ultimates such as cause or first principles. This does not mean that to think in this manner is to think only in metaphysical terms. For, indeed, there is an ontological base in all methodologies. For the contemplative, there is nothing as real as the real world. The difference lies in the person's ability to experience thought. Teaching for contemplation is more than learning by concentration. It is more than the ability to think abstractly. Aristotle believed that contemplation is the practice of the philosopher's peculiar intellectual experience which is called wisdom. There is a suggestion here of perspective. The more a student contemplates the wiser he will become. The wiser he becomes, the more self-sufficient he should become. But contemplation is more than this, it is more than the academic procession from the unknown to the known; it is more than reasoning; it involves meditative experimentation. In this experimentation a logical sequence must be found in every conceptual system in the material of knowledge. It must be rational and coherent and stand the test of experience. Meditative experimentation in its methodology must be coherently constructive in all of its designs and fabrications. It must keep in mind such questions as: What? When? Where? and Why? It moves with an eye on possible solutions but all the time recognizes that alternatives exist and any solution, at best, is but an idea. All of this is a matter requiring thought and contemplation. For in meditative experimentation the learner is reflecting on such things demanded of every scientist, namely, selection and evaluation.

The creative teacher is a provider of a proper learning environment. While environment does not always provide guidelines for learning, it is conducive to thought and contemplation. Thought and contemplation depend to a great extent upon experience and the material of knowledge as well as the learning involvement implicit in all evaluation. To think means the learner is becoming aware of ideas and relationships. Thinking is experiencing a learning activity; it is reasoning and evaluating previous learning technique applying it to the problem being studied.

To *learn* means more than solving a problem; to *study* or determine methodology implies more than the search for data; and to *teach* implies more than the statement of fact. To learn, study or teach requires an intensive use of the imagination. To project a hypothesis is the aim of the imagination. From the carefully structured imagination arises ideas and theories. Theories and ideas suggest designs for activity which can be experienced through the use of meditative experimentation and techniques. Meditative experimentation, the basis of contemplation, requires the use of thorough procedures and techniques, critical and logical in relevancy and application.

To contemplate means the learner possesses a material of knowledge gained through experience. This means that such experience has provided the environment for reflective thought. By the use of reason and imagination the ideas inherent in every fact influence other ideas. Every idea must be based on fact; contemplation is interested in the directives inherent in the scientific method of learning. The scientific method requires a knowledge of logic. To determine truth is to experience its evidence.

Students must dream and structure their dreams intellectually. This is to contemplate a problem and its solution. Contemplation means the objective evaluation of required facts in order to reach a conclusion which is logical and accurate. In contemplation there is a comparative process going on constantly; the learner is comparing theories and ideas which have evolved from his experience with other ideas. The comparison demands there is present an understanding of how two ideas may be similar or different and *why*. Contemplation is a necessary part of the teaching-learning-research process and requires the use of logical reasoning and the making of a value judgment. It is a question of the learner's *willingness* and *ability* to weigh equally all facets of a given problem and understand all factors inherent in the probable solution through experiencing their relationships and relevancy.

— 2 —

The creative teacher realizes that his basic need is to possess the ability to determine the nature of learning.

It is conceivable that today's educator is confused about the nature, scope and purpose of the learning process. It is easy to ask the question: "What is the learning process?" but somewhat more difficult to fully accept current thinking on the subject. There is a questing spirit abroad in our land today; its restlessness stems from its inability to find satisfactory answers to questions about the nature of the learning process.

For instance, there is the fact that the aim of many teachers is to transmit knowledge only. Whose responsibility is it to push back the frontiers of the unknown? For the academician, alert to such a question, there is an unwillingness to permit an instructor to fall prey to but one facet of the learning process. *To do so could betray the responsibility entrusted to its teacher for the learning process.* Moreover, such an attitude toward learning, he will insist, by an instructor would detract from the intrinsic worth, dignity and eminence of the learning process.

There is no division of labor in the learning process. Research and its dissemination are inseparable.

A basic need of the teacher is to possess the ability to determine the nature of learning. Since he already realizes that he must generate perspective in the role he is to play, in order to accomplish this he must be able to determine the exact relationship between learning, teaching, and research. Without this perspective, learning remains impotent and without reason for generation.

This can become something of a problem for the teacher. Generating such a perspective depends upon the determination of relationships. This is an area in which the average teacher is out of practice. While he has a nodding acquaintanceship with the subject of aims and goals and senses that an understanding of interrelationships may aid in their attainment, the *idea* of the *power* inherent in a relationship has made its consideration as an academic connective almost prohibitive. The menacing idea is suggested that all interested people have not understood the philosophical bases of the learning process.

Because of the nature of his role, the creative teacher finds and analyzes the source of the spirit of learning; he is aware of the causative factor in all things and believes that that which *is* possesses a design which can guide and reveal to the learner content and purpose. The creative teacher understands man's source of motivation for learning the *how* and *why* of his drive to comprehend the revelatory powers of truth.

What determines the scope of learning the creative teacher seeks to instill in the thought processes of the learner? Is it the sense of challenge, of knowing the unknown, or the unfolding of promises held out by the discipline of contemplation? It is both a challenge to look for the unknown and its implications and realize that one of its functions is to reveal meaning; the discipline of contemplation is the fulfillment of the thought processes of the learner. To learn *how* to think by understanding its processes and *why* we think as we do because of what the material of knowledge reveals to us suggests that self-realization is the important factor in giving to learning its personal characteristic. Learning must be personal to be meaningful. This premise is based on the following presuppositions. First, the purpose of the created order is the fulfillment of human needs and desires. The aim of all knowledge is to permit the learner to find self-fulfillment. Since self-fulfillment involves the individual, it is more than what Whitehead calls trained intelligence. The learner should not be satisfied with the acquisition of knowledge alone. Self-fulfillment comes with the formulation and expansion of ideas which are found in fact. Second, for the learner to reason about himself and that which is about him is not only to determine his right to certain expectations but to search for an understanding of *how* and *why* these expectations can and should be realized.

The spirit of learning evolves from man's innate power to reason. To know is to comprehend and recognize the implications inherent in the relational pattern existing in every fact. Reason provides direction in the quest for meaning. It is the spirit of learning which provides the learner with the incentive to probe into and develop the meaning of facts and ideas. Such incentive emanates from the innate desire of the learner to fit together the yet uncollected pieces of the unknown. In the process of gaining knowledge a behavior pattern is developed, internal force trends are recognized and new perceptions are elicited by the learner. The learner, then, tends to collect information by bits with the recognized need to fit them into a pattern that is consistent with his values. He experiments with these bits, accepting the one's that can be applied to his value system and which will enable him to gain a greater realization of the potential inherent in a particular fact.

To learn is to recognize the need to handle and control the forces, academic and non-academic alike, exerting potential knowledge upon the person. It is the directives of knowledge which exert external pressures upon the learner. Learning is the response of the activated mind and its spirit to the guideposts for understanding projected by the material of knowledge. What is accepted and used by the mind is taken by its spirit and assimilated by the developing cycle of consciousness found in every philosophy of life.

The cycle of consciousness is an important factor in the psychological make-up of the learner. As a construct it carries with it the realization that learning builds upon previous learning, in a sense, gathering momentum as each fact is added to what is in the process of becoming a whole. An integral part of this process is the developing consciousness which accompanies the comprehension of meaning and understanding. To understand meaning is to be conscious of its application and implication. Learning and its spirit is the originator of the value condition. To place value upon a fact is to find relevancy in that fact; this is its condition. From within the cycle of consciousness the value condition prompts the learner to question the reliability and validity of the material of knowledge. It determines the importance of the subject for the learner. To determine importance is to recognize the applicability of the subject to a personal need. Thus, the spirit of learning motivates and permits the cycle of consciousness to fulfill its purpose.

— 3 —

The creative teacher is aware of the fact that what is of consequence has meaning, and what is learned is believed because it is understood.

The spirit of learning insists that the learner becomes intimately involved in its process. The process is dependent upon the meaning and significance given to the relationship found between parts of its given pattern. From this recognition evolves a methodology which brings with it its own source of motivation. Motivation possesses the skill to develop in the learner an adequate attitude toward the process of learning. Such an attitude includes the value condition and the circumstances necessary to its development.

Learning is transitive in nature, never a complete action or entity. To learn is to experience meaning. Learning takes place when the learner has been motivated by a desire to know and interest has been shown in the unknown. To learn is to become acquainted with the meaning and implications of an idea. This does not mean the student should do nothing but look for ideas. Ideas supply motivation for learning and are suggestive because they invite investigation of what might exist in what now exists in the form of a hint. Ideas open the imagination to the realm of possibility. In the imagination limitations lose their boundaries and act as invitations to explore existents unknown as fact but known by the philosophic mind to having meaning for *is*.

The learning process involves searching for the unknown. To learn is to reach for what now is not being touched. This is the goal of the mind motivated to learn. The learning process involves purpose and method; the use of learning is its own goal. Its vision, structured by aspiration and guided by insight, determines the direction of the reach and its length, the number of pauses to be taken in the process, and the amount of will to be exerted in the effort.

The learning process requires the intense use of concentration. Only aspiration can add this ingredient to the learning process. To say that the degree of intensity required for concentration is determined by interest and motivation is an assumption of the philosophic mind of learning. On the other hand, the self-determining aspect of motivation has as one of its prime purposes to question the validity of aspiration. True vision takes on meaning only when there are other capabilities than enthusiasm present in the learner. While the condition of learning includes the need for this factor, aspiration and its intensity base their right for existence and presence in the process of learning upon their intimate relationship to motivation. Without the reliance which motivation has upon aspiration and intensity, the other pillars in the superstructure of learning, namely, aggregation and assimilation, would be without foundation.

Through concentration and its carefully developed system of analysis, insight is gained into the potential inherent in any object of learning. This is not to say that flashes of insight of learning cannot take place without the intensive use of the powers of concentration, for the creative processes can occur by intuitive means. In the same way the learner may aspire to something never before contemplated. The question, then, is this, "If motivation is not present, what about the validity of the aspiration?"

The learner possesses powers of assimilation which means that he synthesizes and integrates during the process of learning to the degree that his needs are illuminated and his perceptions are sensitized. True learning takes place when motivation and aspiration are present. The learner is able to assimilate through the powers of concentration if the task is meaningful.

Learning (when adequately directed by its spirit) is a simple yet dynamic process based upon motivation, aggregation, assimilation and tempered by the time nexus. With insight, learning takes on what only the impact of understanding can bring to a process. Learning is a continuous process and should not be limited to established facts; rather, there should be a reliance upon the perception gained by transcendent thought as well. Transcendent thought, in attempting to focus the whole picture in order to see relationships, sees experience in terms of it totality, as experience reflects upon itself and its relevancy to fact. By the way of motivation experience directs the learning process to evaluate its findings and, if valid, to project its design through stages of adjustment.

— 4 —

The creative teacher believes that experience serves as the hypothesis of learning.

Experimentation demands a unification of what is known. To force the known upon the unknown is its aim. The unknown reveals itself when its parts are realized and then unified in the learner's mind, seen as a whole and understood in terms of the existing relationship between parts and the parts with the whole. The unification of significant parts into a meaningful whole is an essential aspect of bringing meaning to an ever increasing variety of experience. To learn is to objectify the mind of the unknown and integrate the whole of this model quality with the human mind. It is a connective power possessing the insight which brings into association ideas and facts thereby giving to both their intended meaning. Learning is more that the re-discovery of the established or proven fact. It is a continuous means expanding the *knowing perspective* which includes more than can be seen at the moment or more than can be known in its entirety. Only when the learner is able to collect facts related to an experience and put these facts together into a meaningful whole is he able to change the unknown. Learning involves the extension of the range of the self beyond sensory experience.

Learning requires a sense of commitment to the perspective in inquiry and the values occurring from the process of intellection; it is a commitment to the intellectual development of the learner. Learning is an influence brought to bear upon the data of knowledge; it is the quest for human value and the search for what is morally good. Learning is the development of a sensitivity to the many applicative avenues of value open to rational choice. It is along these avenues that the sense of totality of the learning perspective is seen. Learning is never for its own sake; individuals learn in order to learn more. The learner has a responsibility to the process of learning and the material of knowledge provides for future learning. Every fact suggests value directives. Learning requires the activity of a mind (which is many dimensional in scope) and the use of the will, the nature and purpose of which determines that the learner must place a value upon each item in the educational process.

Facts are *learned* and *perceived* as they stand in relation to each other. In this way insight is gained in the working principles of the material of knowledge. To learn the nature of each fact is to increase the possibility of its mastery. Each fact has both an inner nature as well as external characteristics. Facts become facts because of this nature, and arrive at *becoming* only when given their proper place in a larger schema of meaning.

— 5 —

The creative teacher believes that the learner's conception of understanding determines his desire and will to learn.

This will mean that he has or has not related learning to life and whether or not he looks upon it as a basic process of living. The process of life contends that all of its activities reflect the process of learning. Life is affected by learning; learning equates itself with experience; experience is one continuing feature of life. Learning includes evaluating values and their degree of equality. Learning supplies the drive to achieve quality and, in so doing, achieves purpose. The principle of attainment captures the eye of the potential. To choose an end and a legitimate method to attain it is to learn and create the setting for future learning. Each day the learner encounters the material of knowledge in the form of fact. To look for meaning in that which is separate or seemingly distinct is to understand meaning. Understanding comes when meaning is found in wholes; only the whole of the fact has purpose. We learn for some purpose and this requires the use of introspection. Introspection provides the opportunity for adjustment and revision. Learning remains malleable; at times it suggests modification or the need for qualification.

Learning requires background and preparation; it is attentive to operative relationships within the whole of the knowledge structure. Learning recognizes its need to maintain a perspective of the contours of the design and its adequacies or inadequacies. Out of perspective arises the ability to think; by means of thought the learner is able to test the design and its purpose for its functional attributes. In this way the ability to conceptualize is born. Every problem carries with it a general idea. To conceptualize that idea will mean the formulation of new settings, and within these new settings, new experiences.

Ideas rely on one another; the learner can compare their attributes and characteristics. An extension of one idea may become the germ of another idea. The important criterion of coherence of purpose is established when ideas move toward a common aim. Learning means that communication has been established with an idea. Ideas form conceptual patterns of thought; such designs generate techniques for the mastery of content. Techniques in learning supply the base to which attitudes can return for clarification; from techniques arise skills and the *habit* to learn.

— 6 —

The creative teacher believes that scholarship is a quality of being and a state of becoming.

Intellectual depth is more than a quality of fact. Scholarship is more than *what* is gained by structuring or disciplining the process of learning or achieving depth in reading or study. Scholarship always poses a problem for the inquiring mind; it wants to know the significance and implications of meaning. Too often scholarship is defined by pointing to its results or the nature of its quality. Just as there is a difference in the meaning between words *knowing* and knowledge, there is a difference between the concepts *learning* and *scholarship*.

A number of questions might be raised about the academic and professional qualifications of the individual aspiring to a life of scholarship. They are five in number. What characteristic traits of learning are not characteristic of scholarship? What academic principle is at work here, if such a distinction can be made? As one pursues the role of the scholar is the search for knowledge his ultimate aim? Does this mean that knowledge is sought for its own sake? Has knowledge goals inherent in its nature?

The realization of the learning process is achieved in part because of a basic demand of scholarship. The demand is for honesty in motivation, thinking, creativity and in the problems of semantics (demanding a consistency which projects meaning in the use of language). This does not delimit the use of the word semantics even when it is recognized that meanings may be differently interpreted and still be honest. Honesty is always subject to assumption; the test of its validity is the recognition of its relevancy when it is realized that often assumptions based on experience alone are biased and may be filled with value feelings. The demand means honesty in raising questions which are valid and meaningful and have their base in fact. It means honesty in the use of ideas, recognizing their potential as well as their limitations.

Learning would lose its dignity if its concept of scholarship is limited to the idea that scholarship is equated with a methodology designed for the acquisition of knowledge alone. The mind does not serve as a place of storage for the accumulation of facts and details of these facts, nor does it seek only to transmit to each new generation these same facts. Scholarship includes this responsibility, but much more. These are not presuppositions, starting points in understanding the role and the responsibility of scholarship. Methodology is not an end unto itself, but a means; it has accepted the premise that, to extend the limits of knowledge other means or levels such as the use of abstract thought are needed.

All knowledge has subjective value, both in meaning and in relevancy. This is the same as saying that all things have a personal meaning. Knowledge is more than the recognition of the fact by the scholar. A fact exists because of its possibilities for use as a value condition which suggests the true purpose of the fact. It is the value condition which unites one fact with another. This is the purpose which the creative teacher projects through his responsibility in the realm of scholarship. And yet he is not unique in holding this position. For the value a learner assigns to a fact involves the recognition of the fact in relation to personal and individual needs. An essential attribute of all human knowing is the *value* placed upon things. True purpose cannot exist without regard to a value condition. The value condition determines how the fact is used objectively and subjectively. The value condition does not find itself arbitrarily assigned to knowledge.

The *whole* of learning is created and brought into being as a product of the creative mind when two or more proven facts unite and give birth to a new life. To be aware that new life (or a thing) has come into being is not sufficient knowledge to project by means of facts. Facts in themselves cannot produce new life, but it is the idea which interprets the facts and related them which furnish the material to bind them together to form a new substance. Thus, being aware of a thing for the first time is not sufficient reason to ascribe it to the realm of fact; rather there is the need to see if proof of existence can be established. To understand the potential of new life when it is properly motivated and to interpret its structure in its natural setting is to approach the aim of scholarship, namely, the actualization of meaning in the learning disciplines. To achieve meaning is to understand; this includes having a grasp of possibilities when fully explored.

Scholarship is concerned with methodology. But the question of selecting method and skills for processing the material of knowledge is an area too often neglected. Moreover, dedication to a specialization which is at the expense of what only the perspective of generalization can bring to a problem, fails to give scholarship the disciplinary strength by the scholar. In the same way, dedication to a generalization which is at the expense of what only the delimited perspective of specialization can bring to a problem, fails to give scholarship the disciplinary strength needed by the scholar. Excessive specialization at the expense of generalizations or the development of broad principles tends to limit the realization of the potential extensions of knowledge.

Scholarship is difficult to define because it possesses a mystic and perhaps a cryptic element. It is elusive for it is possible that a student who is an expert in research is not a scholar. Such a person has not learned how to think or create. Scholarly attainment comes only with the mind's motivation. Scholarship is achieved where the mind has been thoroughly oriented in ways other than specialization. Scholarship is an attitude developed only when the mind has been disciplined in methods of communication. To handle information is not the only quest of scholarship. Nor is it the demand for excellence, or is it adequate to say that the scholar "seeks for truth" as though the search for truth or the truth itself is the end product of the educational process. The key to scholarship lies within the mind's attitude toward learning. Clear thinking, for instance, can become one resultant of the learning process; in its development it can become scholarly in the methodology and perspective. Clear thinking should make possible the achievement of a closer approximation of the truth.

Scholarship resists the temptation to accept as truth what is only partially seen or understood; it refuses to accept half-truths. But can scholarship exist if something is accepted which cannot be proved? Is all truth at best only partially understood? If this is the case, the whole of a problem can never fully be realized; the best one can do is to strive for as much understanding as possible under the limitations of the circumstances and as warranted by them. This would say that the scholar must accept half-truths because truth is only relative.

The word *compromise* is not found in the vocabulary used by scholarship. Therefore, honesty, which presupposes an open mind is one of the most important attributes of the scholar. Honesty implies that the scholar is in control of his biases. The scholar knows how to use his bias; therefore, he recognizes that it is one of his strongest motivating factors. Often the scholar seeks to validate a theory partially formed by bias. However, he will accept new ideas and relationships even though they may invalidate his personal theory. This is not to say that contemplation has no justification. The scholar does not say "I think" or "I am of the opinion" but rather he supports a hypothesis, equated with a theory, flexes his methodological muscles, always ready to analyze, step by step, the leads supplied by insight gained through observation. Contemplation evidences itself in theory and is recognized as such by the scholar. A theory is an opinion to be validated by observation and experimentation.

The function of experience is important to the scholar. Experience is a personal thing. Communication takes place by way of experience. Communication means that an exchange of ideas is taking place; this is a form of experience. The desire to learn and understand evolves from experience. Communication is the interaction of inquiring minds; it is investigation; it prepares the stage for learning. Learning is one form of experience. Communication, the outgrowth of experience, provides the creative energy necessary for the generation of ideas. Ideas are mandatory for the growth of the mind and always suggest change.

The pivot about which scholarship revolves is vision. It seeks new birth and change; innovation serves as its source of motivation. Patterns of thought that characterize an inquisitive spirit at work in the mind are indicative of scholarship's explorative nature. Its drive is for continuous learning growth toward self-realization and the actualization of meaning and the value condition.

Scholarship depends upon the nature of the relationship among mind, method and the material of knowledge. Scholarship is the product of mental activity; it depends upon the sense of direction provided by method and the *sense* of experimentation programmed by the mind. The scholar learns because of what the material of learning opens to him and the interaction of his previous experience with new ideas; he is stimulated to learn by what is afforded by the material of knowledge.

Scholarship and creative ability go hand in hand. Scholarship means that a high degree of perception has been attained and the analytical senses have been sharpened, not for the sake of technical ability but rather for the controls which are used to determine learning potential. The scholar views the unknown with a sense of caution. Learning is horizontal in structure, not levels or layers but merging steps, each dependent upon the other for momentum. Scholarship does not exist only to add to knowledge, nor does it bespeak the formalities of education. Scholarship begins at the place where a validated conceptualization of the idea gives way to the synthesization of its application.

One of the mistaken notions with respect to the responsibility of the scholar is that he must arouse the intellect for learning. Nonsense says the mind of scholarship; this is the responsibility of the material of knowledge. To study the mind of knowledge and its material is the function of scholarship.

Scholarship has as one of its many presuppositions the belief that mind and the material of knowledge are strands in the weave of the created order of all things. Mind is an integral part of the nature of knowledge; it can never be separated from the object of its inquiry.

It is not the learning process that assures the learner of gaining *so much* knowledge; rather, it is the mind of the learner and knowledge which is most essential to scholarship. The goal of the scholar resides in the mind. Methodology is based upon the nature, scope and purpose of the aim. It is this relationship alone which permits the scholar to recognize the implications of what he has learned. The material of knowledge has a way of testing the findings and results of the scholar and doing so by the methods and aims he has projected. In a sense, the material of knowledge forces the researcher to answer questions about the self and the attitude which is brought to the research problem. In other words, he must be able to explain each step taken in the process of drawing his conclusions. Thus the researcher must conceptualize his findings and test the logic of his thought processes.

— 7 —

The creative teacher believes that knowledge, while pursued by the learner, is hard on its own pursuit, namely, the integration of its own material in the human mind.

That which is gained by knowing, knowledge and understanding, is the resultant of the conceptualization of the material of knowledge as well as the application of ideas to theories. Knowledge is interested in the integrated mind; it wants to understand the implications of the relationships found in every fact. Intellectual integration is an attribute enhancing the dignity of the learning process.

While knowledge will determine the validity of a fact, each fact possesses many assumptions or presuppositions. Each fact is realized, in part, by some method based on assumptions. A new discovery may disprove what was accepted as a fact. The method, as each step has been taken, has brought its logic with it; its own language has fostered a mode of thought forced by its purpose to be functional. And yet, even though method and language may be peculiar to the structure of the fact, the implications of the fact through its relationship to other facts receives its coloration from its relevancy to a whole. When substantive coloring has been received, meaning for the part as well as for the whole has been actualized. Thus, a fact cannot stand alone and possess a value as a fact. The learner seeks to attain an understanding of the relationship between facts, integrating them into an unified whole.

While it is sometimes difficult to be certain of an implication, as well as academically secure in the premise there has been a divorce between attitude and feeling, scholarship must be based on the integration of knowledge. Herein intellection provides meaning for what has been learned.

Meaning arises from experience and is never complete until integration is achieved. We can say, then, that every fact has a functional purpose and because of its nature exists to answer a question or solve a problem. A fact for the sake of itself does not exist in the learning process. Facts call forth new relationships which are consistent with their inter-relationships. Facts suggest ideas; this activity is the process of integrating knowledge. It is not the process of taking the whole of knowledge and relating it to the whole of its material of content. Or, is it the process of relating the whole of a discipline to the whole of another discipline? It is the process of permitting (maybe even forcing) a fact to react upon yet another fact, idea or theory in order to determine relevancy for application to the problem under study.

Knowledge must be experienced in order to be assimilated. It can be a vicarious experience; in a sense it is a basic demand of knowledge. It carries within itself, both in its entirety and within its parts, an organization structured to reveal its content. Knowledge cannot be accepted as an end product alone, nor is the pursuit of it limited to the methodologies of learning.

Knowledge reveals a methodology for the unfolding of its material to the human mind through its nature. An intrinsic organization of knowledge exists even though knowledge seems to be completely dependent upon facts and is subjected to interpretation through careful analysis of their content. It is a developmental process, properly correlated to reveal every facet of its structure. In this way knowledge is unfolded by the human mind. The experience of the mind provides meaning which is reflected by the material of knowledge. In this way the creative teacher says that all knowledge possesses an intrinsic organization of its material.

The learner does not add to his knowledge; he develops it through the extension and expansion of its directives. Knowledge requires in its learner the skill of a weaver; there are strands (each dependent upon another for strength) of proven fact which can prove suggestive of other facts as yet unrealized. The material of knowledge possesses a pattern; many complex strands of fact (a series of connected and related facts) are needed to reveal design and meaning. To sense the associative and dependent qualities inherent in every strand of fact is to possess the ability to integrate knowledge. Insight into these dependency factors guarantees the learner an experience of assimilation. As knowledge grows, it develops.

To integrate knowledge is to perceive the relationship and re-sponsibility of fact to fact and to bring into focus (actualizing) their associative qualities. To actualize is to bring into being; it is done by the perceiver even though the relationship already exists. On this basis the learner begins to develop his ability to conceptualize the idea.

Knowledge embodies the known and the existent of all associative factors of each. The material of knowledge exists outside of the learner; while the learner may not know the associative factors of each bit of knowledge, he strives for an understanding of these rela-tionships. An associative factor is a connective link and might be said to be the mutual property of knowledge. Knowledge does not recog-nize the validity of an isolated fact. Facts, for meaning, are de-pendent upon inter-relationships among ideas. To sense and thereby reason or intuit these relationships is to experience integrative thought. It is the kind of thing which can be done only by the individual learner. He must experience it as his mind functions ac-cording to the stimulation and direction provided by knowledge it-self. Thus, knowledge, for the sake of the learner furnishes directives for the understanding of its material.

To develop discriminatory powers by means of perception is an integral part of the learning process. Every learner is a reactor to what is before him to be learned. Knowledge confronts the learner with its material; this is another way of saying that the learner is confronted with the material of knowledge. To evaluate critically and with accuracy the learner must possess the ability to discriminate between facts and their relevancy to a problem. The learner must find the answers to such questions as: When is a fact a fact? When is a fact relevant and complete? Earlier it was suggested that a fact can never be fully comprehended and that *knowing* includes a process of gaining a comprehension of its meaning in its relation to other facts. This does not imply a state of finality. For instance, if the learner rejects a fact as irrelevant, the question is whether or not he has discovered its true design, intention and function. A second would then be raised: Is it possible for a fact to be relevant without de-termining its completeness?

To determine when a fact is relevant is to determine its complete-ness. The intention and design of the fact is found in its complete-ness. Only the scholarly mind uses its discriminatory powers to properly integrate its knowledge and makes certain that its assump-tions are correct.

All knowledge points out to the learner his need to adjust to change. Knowledge seen only in part demands of the learner the need to adjust and see the relation of the particular to the whole. *Knowledge then, seen only in part, is indeed knowledge, but to see in part is to understand imperfectly.* Knowledge is aware that its parts, to be meaningful, interact with other parts of itself, and parts with wholes. Integration of knowledge takes place when there is this interaction between parts and with wholes. Thus the character of knowledge causes the learner to be aware of his need to adjust to change. Knowledge seen only in part causes the learner to see the need to adjust to and see the relation of the part to the whole. Knowledge, to be meaningful, must be seen in terms of its interaction with other parts and parts with wholes. Integration of knowledge takes place when this interaction between parts and with wholes is perceived.

The object of integrative thought is not knowledge. Integrative thought is achieved when knowledge has been experienced; knowledge and its material brings it into being through its methodology. It is the way knowledge insists that its material is processed by the mind that determines the validity of integration.

Integrative knowledge is not as interested in the learner's search for knowledge as it is in the way its content is handled, applied and utilized.

Integrative thought is a cumulative process. This does not mean that the learner is able to think because he has accumulated a great many ideas. Though this is essential, it does not necessarily mean that satisfaction is gained by filling each idea with a great many facts. Accumulation of ideas may not force one into the formulation of new ideas, but it contributes to the generative powers of the mind. It is integrative thought which causes the learner to sense the need for change, if necessary, in the blending process of learning. Integrative thought is creative in action for it uses the material of knowledge to determine new learning perspectives.

Mental activity implies reactive behavior; for the mind to function it must react. Thinking means there is a reaction to an idea, theory or fact. Thinking is reflection for it experiences the idea. To react is to conceptualize; this ability permits the learner to theorize. In other words, he becomes conscious of what the material of knowledge seeks to reveal to him.

There is a precision found in nature. Likewise this is true with respect to knowledge. The first thing knowledge seeks to reveal to the learner is its precision. This is seen in the cellular organizational patterns of its material. The integration of knowledge is a process like the growth of its cellular organizational structure. It comes into existence when the parts are seen in relation to the whole and the mind reflects upon the change which takes place in the resultant interactivity within the process of learning.

— 8 —

The creative teacher believes that the learner, in reacting to theory and fact, must draw certain conclusions and make a number of decisions. He believes that new and unsuspected relationships will evolve from this perception of theory and fact.

Perception cannot be gained without drawing conclusions and making decisions. To perceive, the learner must possess more than the design of a theory of the material of the fact; he must see each in its proper setting and within that setting gain a perspective involving inter-relationships between particulars. To gain this kind of perspective is one of the most difficult processes of intellection. Perspective has an intellectual power peculiar to itself; it is a power tempered by wisdom. It suggests that an infinite number of relationships come into being as each change is realized by the learner. The perception of change is understood only in its relational setting. True intellection insists that it is not possible to see things in terms of their relationships and at the same time to be unaware whether these things are true or false. To gain perspective is a mental process; it is the process of intellection; it is the proper use of the intellect.

Intellection, as a value condition of the learning process, makes learning meaningful. Its purpose is to understand the nature of the self-determinative process of learning, the implications of change demanded by knowledge, the significance of contradiction in the material of knowledge, and the myth surrounding the supposed need for the learner to adjust to his environment. The directives of learning are inherent in the material of knowledge.

While it is true that the learner often seeks an environment to which he wishes to adjust and just as often finds it necessary to adjust to a situation not to his liking, to such circumstances intellection addresses itself; the aim of intellection is to develop a means of mental control over environment. The control of reality is the task of intellection.

Intellection, as a pivot of the learning process, requires the learner to recognize his dependency upon fundamental principles in the area of the value condition and accept the premise that such a condition is not determined by flexible goals alone.

The learning process concerns the effect knowledge has upon the learner. In this way it can be said that education is *used* to stimulate and guide the self-development of the student. The learning activity which involves the effect that the material of knowledge has upon the learner is another way of bringing this learning principle to the front. Such an effect projects the change which takes place in the learning process. A change which bespeaks stability is recognized as a product of the activity suggested here as intellection. Thus, its aim is to control the change assumed to take place because of learning; to give change direction and stability is its avowed purpose. Change is instituted through knowledge; to promote change intellection permits the recognition of principles and their acceptance for use in the process.

Change requires resources. These must be identified and paralleled with the learner's need. Change requires meaning in experience. Meaning is found only in the value condition. This condition is never pre-determined *for* the learner but is pre-determined *by* the learner. This is the setting in which intellection sees itself operating most effectively.

Intellection recognizes that the opinions or beliefs of individuals many times are based on bias; intellection warns the mind of the learner against a dependency upon opinion. Unsound interpretations and unanalyzed motives have no place in the function of intellection.

It is true, of course, that certain types of experience are de-termined *for* the learner. But it is the force of the value condition which changes the inherent direction of the learning process at this junction. The value that the learner places on such experience is thus pre-determined. And, even such pre-determination is often in-fluenced by the manner in which the experience is realized. In a sense, then, pre-conditioning in the learner can cause the value condi-tion to be so pre-determined that its direction can be predicted.

The resultant of the interaction between intellection and knowl-edge is understanding. Understanding is provided for through mean-ing; it does not exist apart from meaning. Knowledge is attained with the insight gained from understanding.

Intellection concerns itself with the unconscious assumptions in-herent in every facet of the learning process. It seeks for the clarifica-tion of thought patterns inherent in every presupposition. It estab-lishes the need to define each presupposition in terms of its nature as an inferential construct. This is done by means of its power to inte-grate experience. Creative teachers can influence the value condition placed on experience by a student. In the same way, a course of study can take on an entirely different meaning when handled by another instructor.

Experience infers further experience and insight as well as refines and sharpens the inquiring mind; it prepares the mind to profit from its experiences and see itself in perspective as it becomes sensitive to its own potential and ideas. Such sensitivity guides the mind in its self-discipline and the articulation of its method for critical thinking.

The source of all knowledge is experience. The more meaningful the experience the sharper will be the thought. Concern must be shown then in making a distinction between facts and the interpretation of facts. Even if the creative teacher is unable to structure the value condition, in most cases he will be able to determine the type of experience which will open the fact for study. Intellection is concerned with assumptions; meaning is achieved through experiencing the fact.

— 9 —

The creative teacher believes that bias is a natural trait arising from the human tendency to be prejudicial in one's learnings, academic and non-academic alike. Therefore, the learning process, to preserve its dignity, must insist that its learner's recognize bias for what it is, a bent intellection.

Unstructured, incomplete and meaningless experiences often give birth to bias. It is the learner's responsibility to recognize bias as an incomplete experience; without the ability to evaluate and control bias the learner will find it impossible to pursue intellectual activity.

To be prejudicial is to judge; bias is a conclusion based upon a value condition. It is an attitude based upon a subjective and emotional response to the unknown; the object of bias is never known completely and has not been studied objectively. Bias comes into being when an inadequate evaluation has been made; it receives its directives and controls from the uncertainty found in half-truths. Uncertainty arises because conclusions have been drawn on unproved assumptions.

The creative teacher insists that his learner see into all causative elements in fact and be able to rightly appraise the value conditions arising from cause itself. Each fact contains structured data; this must serve as a basis for thought. To see in data the probable or potential, structured objectively and systematically is to follow a guide, purposive in intent, bent on revealing new knowledge. In such a perspective there is no room for bias and prejudice in the learning process.

— 10 —

The value condition is an asset as well as a personal liability evolving from the learning process. Value is a personal obligation that stems from learning. In this emphasis placed upon obligation the teacher suggests that the learner knows why he holds the values he does and whether there is the possibility that some values are based upon bias.

The creative teacher is saying here that all value is contingent upon the purposive activity of learning and, therefore, is relative. Its status, however, can become absolute while remaining a condition. This is the kind of paradox permitted in conceptual thought. The condition presupposes the actualization of a moral precept when the status symbol is absolute. In other words, it is the actualization of a value. Value and fact become equated in this way in the absolute sense; however, value remains a condition based on fact until the involved precept becomes actualized by the learner. The value condition is based on fact found in all of life's situations; it maintains a constant reference to fact as it has been actualized in the realm of thought. Ideas of what constitutes reality come from this source and provides the learner with a sense of direction in his quest for knowledge. The value condition concerns itself with what *is* and *what should be*. Even what is relative refers to what *is*. What is relative presupposes an ability of the learner to interpret what may exist only for the sake of transfer. What *is* refers to both segments of existence, the absolute and the relative. This dichotomy exists in conceptual thought.

Value is conditioned by its dependency upon integrity. Integrity suggests completeness in a fact; without it the fact is rendered meaningless. Values are found in the material of knowledge and are never assumed. Conditioned for existence by the learner, theory and fact become a value construct. Values, whether formulated or discovered, are determined by the mind. It is an internal process and decision with moral implications. Values cannot be imposed or legislated; whatever system may be established is structured by the way facts establish themselves as sets in the mind. A set is an established pattern of belief, changed only as fact and theory shift emphasis or give way to new and more significant facts and theories. The recognition of the relevancy of a fact establishes itself in the learning process as a value condition. The value is conditioned by its utility and applicative connotation as well as by its esthetic qualities. Conformity to the directive of any fact is not only suggestive of acceptance but a recognition of its utility. To imitate a fact is to value it sufficiently to actualize it.

Value is experiential in meaning. As the perceptions of experience change, values change. Attitudes are synonymous with the value condition; this does not suggest the subjectiveness rather than the absoluteness of values. Value is conditioned by the validity of perception, the depth of attitudes and the nature of the learning perspective.

Valuation, including appraisal and estimation, is the philosophical mind of science at work. Valuation is a science because it is experimental in its objectivity, and its frame of reference is found in the material of knowledge. Both appraisal and estimation connote an exactness of breadth and scope indicative of the perspective of the scientific method. Since valuation insists that its method is objective, a value cannot be based wholly upon a sensual reaction such as an emotion. Value, as a discovery, brings into being controls for actualizing each finding. To value is to find meaning in relationships.

Value is fully conscious of the many implications of fact. Value realizes that its attitude and stance must conform and agree with the meaning and signification of fact; this means recognizing the truth inherent in fact. While personal values are determined by the mind, the condition of what to value rests with the content of fact itself.

Because value is a condition, it is subject to change. The ideal, in order to maintain its stance must continue to grow; its perspective must increase and sharpen. This requires a basic reliance upon fact as a starting point in the responsibility of finding a value condition. Reliance upon fact permits perspective to be functional; every fact possesses a value potential; this determines end or purpose. Progress is based largely upon the condition of value.

Value concerns itself with quality. Quality is a resultant of completed purpose. Purpose is based upon ethical and moral principles, and demands of the learner a decision as to its relevancy. With a decision of this type, purpose claims the right to commitment. Thus purpose carries within its aim a methodology based upon a value condition.

All value is conditioned because it is based on a belief in measurement. Measurement bespeaks quantity as well as quality; in this sense the structure of value is said to be measurement. The learner values what has been measured for importance and significance. Furthermore, value is conditioned because its measurement is applicable to the individual alone. What is of value to one person may not be of value to another. There can be no price *fixing* of value; each learner must set his own price. As a condition of fact, value recognizes its own need for adjustment. This is one of the most workable traits of the value condition.

Fact, by means of its purpose, provides value with direction. Value is realized when the learner thinks deeply about what is important to him. The potential of each fact is realized in this way. The value condition has power to transform an idea into reality and a fact into a quality. The conscious reaction of the learner to what has qualitative significance for him makes of the value condition functional in purpose; its objective is judgmental satisfaction.

— 11 —

The question is one of the most important facets of the learning process. To understand its potential, the creative teacher insists that the learner acquaint himself with the internal and external characteristics of a well-structured, highly motivated question.

The creative teacher is concerned not only with the methodology of a question but with its content and perspective. Methodology is a product of the learning experience and not the main objective of the question.

The question is based upon three factors: the basic idea, a fact related to the idea, and the complete idea. It is the idea which prompts the learner to question. The question implies that the learner has observed but has failed to understand completely what he has seen; he has experienced in part but has failed to understand the implications of what he has sensed. The complete idea projects the necessity of knowing the relatedness of the answer or fact to other materials of knowledge. There are degrees of understanding. Every idea involves some understanding of a fact and its implications.

The question looks for verification and is based upon the potential projected by the idea; it is verification alone that brings complete understanding. The idea, related to the experience of the learner, arises from the directives emanating from fact. The idea will have little potential unless the learner recognizes these directives and what they imply. Basically, the question is founded upon principles already determined by what *is*.

The learner must realize, says the creative teacher, that inherent in every question is method and the need to reason. The question is dependent upon the learner's ability to develop ideas through his power to reason and the ability of the mind to search for the answer *why*. The learner *in* and *by* the question seeks to examine and test what begins as a theory. To develop a theory one must recognize an implication; the question is an attempt to verify an implication. The learner's objective is to permit the fact to actualize itself in his mind. Since all facts suggest inferences, in reality they are suggesting the need to question. Since all facts suggest the need for perception, in reality they are suggesting the need for apprehension. All of this calls for something more than what is found in the mind of the learner. Memory recall is not sufficient motivation for the total question. While it is agreed that memory is fundamental to the learning process and stems from the ability to reason (the primary object of the process) to question means an acceptance of the learner's need to explain by way of definition and analysis, the fact.

The question presupposes the proven past of the fact. In order for the question to be adequate it must give evidence of a logical order; the thought inherent in a question demands a consistency in its natural progression toward realization. There must be the kind of thought in every question which controls potentiality and the development of a concept conducive to further discovery. The question then is a part of the reasoning process.

Thought is stimulated and permitted to hold in check, until verified, potential answers. The true question is the creative part of the reasoning process because it works through the use of concepts. It concerns itself with the ability of the material of knowledge to reveal itself through the process of abstraction. In every question the assumed *why?* demands an answer. To this end it prepares itself to reason.

The power to reason is to possess the power to infer. All inference is in need of controls; only the use of perception possesses the insight necessary to direct inference to be a useful guide in the learning process and the development of an answer.

The question is an integral part of the thought process and its preparation should involve the use of the scientific method. The properly structured question will enable the researcher to experience his findings; it is a conscious effort involving all the intellectual forces of the learner. The content of every question should be based upon knowledge already gained. The question exists to permit the learner to experience in depth the unfolding process revealed by the material of knowledge; it brings with it the power for concentration.

To question is to be faced with a new learning problem. To question is to ask *why?* and discover the *what* and *how*. The *what* and *how* must be based on the learner's experience and his ability to

relate his experiences. To question is to create an interaction between the unknown and the learner's mind; it is to create an experience. To question is to reinforce experience with the quest for new
ideas; it is to reconstruct the past and combine the future's inference
with the associative ideas emanating from the merger of the proven
and the perspective. To question is to be sensitive to the ideas emanating from the material of knowledge; it is the ability to comprehend the meaning and signification of the properties of knowledge
and to sense the implications of a projected proposition.

Questioning prepares the setting for intellectual growth. It serves
to stimulate experience and bring into being one of the most potent
forces in higher learning, namely, awareness of inferences inherent in
new relationships between theory and fact.

The responsibility of the question is to test the concept.

— 12 —

*The creative teacher believes that the fragmentation of the cur-
riculum has done more to destroy learning's dynamic cycle of consciousness than any other factor in its structure.*

The creative teacher insists that his learners possess an integrative
perspective of the world. The academic diaspora, caused by fragmentation has not given the learning process the universality of out-
look so necessary to its health. It is fragmentation which destroys the
potentiality of scholarship. Knowledge is a unified whole and not a
collection of isolated facts.

Fragmentation of the curriculum or the departmentalization of
the material of knowledge is but one aspect of the problem. While it
is recognized that departmentalization does not necessarily mean
fragmentation, instruction is the key to the continuation and relating
of units of knowledge contained in relationships. Likewise, to draw a
distinction between general and specialized education, suggesting perhaps that the former serves as a preparation for the latter, is to
by-pass the symptoms of a deeper source of academic disease. And
yet it is readily admitted that knowledge is expanding in all areas and
fields, so that the question is raised as to the necessity of specializing
in order to fully understand any fraction of one field of knowledge.
Or, perhaps the real question to ask is whether or not knowledge can
be packaged and artificially isolated into subjects or departments by
means of the learner's scapel. The case against fragmentation of the
curriculum or the departmentalization of knowledge is, in reality, the
case against the restrictive perspective, methodology and appli-

cability of disciplines integrated by nature, scope and purpose. And yet there seems to be the need to dissect the body of knowledge into units or parts to be learned in a given setting and within a given time. Fragmentation does not create scholarship. Rather, it undermines its aims even though a learner may have the ability for creativeness in the area in which he plans to specialize. Fragmentation does not bring together related disciplines and proffer the perspective insisted upon by scholarship; it destroys horizons of higher learning and it is unnatural to the complete and integrated learning process.

Integrative thought accepts the premise that the curricula in education must be flexible and diversified, but it does not accept the belief that learning is to be based on the trivium and quadrivium. Fragmentation destroys the integrative core of education, namely, what is universal in its nature.

Is it possible to facilitate research without specializing? Fragmentation is isolationism. When one subject or area is taught as an entity or as a fact entirely apart from its supporting fields (and every fact has supporting facts) the disease of academic isolationism has set in.

All human action is based on thought which stems not from the isolated fact but rather from the whole of knowledge. Fragmentation of thought assumes that the task of education is to transmit accumulated knowledge rather than be concerned with the learning process. Fragmentation places the content of education first on the academic agenda rather than its process. Content without its process and design remains but unrelated fact. The process of education alone guarantees growth in learning. Thought itself, while it can be selective, cannot be fragmented. All thought is of an educative nature; it strives for unity and integration. Thought implies an awareness of organic perspective; it cannot be limited to an area designated as a discipline or course of study. Thought, by its very nature, is interdisciplinary in scope and purpose.

$$- 13 -$$

Who, then, is the creative teacher?

The creative teacher rejects the belief that the mind is but a receptor of knowledge and ideas. He believes the learner must be involved in the learning process in order to be creative and find meaning in any area of learning. The material of knowledge, as acted upon by the mind, acts upon the mind as well and is not a segmented entity. The material of knowledge requires a universality of purpose which crosses subject area lines. Fragmentation bespeaks artificiality; it does not exist in thought or in the nature of the created order.

The creative teacher believes that learning means more than the mastery of a table of contents, itemized because the academic disciplines are considered as entities.

The creative teacher organizes the learning experience in such a way that what is being learned is at the same time being applied to some facet of life's experiential values.

Bibliography

E.L. Allen, *Existentialism from Within*, Routledge and Kegan Paul, Ltd.

Gordon W. Allport, *Becoming: Basic Considerations for a Psychology of Personality*, Yale University Press.

H. Anderson, editor, *Creativity and Its Cultivation*, Harper and Row.

Aristotle, *The Complete Works*, W.D. Ross, translator, Random House.

Francis Bacon, *Advancement of Learning and Novum Organum*, edited by J. Creighton, Colonial Publishing, Inc.

William Barrett, *Irrational Man*, Doubleday.

———, *What is Existentialism?*, Grove Press.

Frank Barron, *Creative Person and Creative Process*, Holt, Rinehart and Winston, Inc.

N. Berdyaev, *The Meaning of the Creative Act*, Harper and Row.

George Berkeley, *Principles of Human Knowledge*, Bobbs-Merrill.

H.J. Blackham, *Six Existentialist Thinkers*, Harper Torchbooks.

J.S. Brubacher, *Modern Philosophies of Education*, McGraw-Hill Book Co.

J.S. Bruner, *On Knowing*, Belknap Press.

———, *Toward A Theory of Instruction*, W.W. Norton and Company, Inc.

Martin Buber, *I and Thou*, Scribner's.

———, *Between Man and Man*, Beacon Press.

Albert Camus, *The Myth of Sisyphus*, Knopf.

———, *The Plague*, Knopf.

———, *The Rebel*, Knopf.

———, *Resistance, Rebellion, and Death*, Knopf.

———, *The Stranger*, Vintage Books.

O.F. Clarke, *Introduction to Berdyaev*, Geoffrey Bles.

J. Collins, *The Existentialists*, Regnery.

L.A. Cremin, *The Transformation of the School*, Knopf.

Wilfred Desan, *The Tragic Finale: An Essay on the Philosophy of Jean-Paul Sartre*, Harper Torchbooks.

Rene Descartes, *The Philosophical Works*, Dover, Two volumes.

John Dewey, *How We Think*, D.C. Heath.

———, *The Child and the Curriculum*, University of Chicago Press.

Fyodor Dostoevsky, *The Brothers Karamazov*, Modern Library.

Marvin Farber, *The Aims of Phenomenology*, Harper Torchbooks.

———, *Phenomenology and Existence*, Harper Torchbooks.

J.W. Getzels and P.W. Jackson, *Creativity and Intelligence*, John Wiley and Sons, Inc.

Brewster Ghiselin, editor, *The Creative Process*, New American Library.

John Curtis Gowan, editor, Creativity: *Its Educational Implications*, John Wiley and Sons, Inc.

M. Greene, *Dreadful Freedom*, University of Chicago Press.

———, *Existential Encounters for Teachers*, Random House.

E.F. Hammer, *Creativity*, Random House.

R. Harper, *Existentialism: A Theory of Man*, Harvard University Press.

Martin Heidegger, *Discourse on Method*, Harper and Row.

———, *Existence and Being*, Regnery.

———, *An Introduction to Metaphysics*, Yale University Press.

F.H. Heinemann, *Existentialism and the Modern Predicament*, Harper Torchbooks.

David Hume, *A Treatise on Human Nature*, Oxford.

E. Husserl, *Phenomenology and the Crisis of Philosophy*, Harper Torchbooks.

E.D. Hutchinson, *How to Think Creatively*, Abingdon Press.

William James, *The Will to Believe*, Dover.

Karl Jaspers, *Man in the Modern Age*, George Routledge and Sons.

———, *The Way to Wisdom*, Yale University Press.

Jerome Kagan, editor, *Creativity and Learning*, Beacon Press.

Immanuel Kant, *Critique of Pure Reason*, A Doubleday Anchor Book.

F.R. Karl and L. Hamalian, editors, *The Existential Imagination*, A Fawcett Premier Book.

Soren Kierkegaard, *The Present Age*, Harper Torchbooks.

———, *Sickness Unto Death*, Anchor Books.

W.H. Kilpatrick, *Philosophy of Education*, Macmillan.

George F. Kneller, *Existentialism and Education*, John Wiley and Sons, Inc.

John Locke, *An Essay Concerning Human Understanding*, Dover, Two volumes.

Gabriel Marcel, *Being and Having*, Harper Torchbooks.

———, *Homo Viator*, Harper Torchbooks.

———, *The Philosophy of Existentialism*, Citadel Press.

J. Maritain, *Existence and the Existent*, Pantheon.

A.H. Maslow, *Towards a Psychology of Being*, D. Van Nostrand.

Rollo May, editor, *Existential Imagination*, Random House.

Peter McKellar, *Imagination and Thinking*, Basic Books.

J.S. Mill, *A System of Logic*, Longmans, Green and Co., Inc.

Van Cleve Morris, *Existentialism and Education*, Harper and Row.

A.F. Osborn, *Applied Imagination*, Scribner's.

———, *Creative Imagination*, Scribner's.

Plato, *Works of Plato*, Loeb Classical Library, William Heinenmann.

C.R. Rogers, *On Becoming a Person*, Houghton Mifflin Co.

Bertrand Russell, *The Analysis of Mind*, Macmillan.

———, *Human Knowledge, Its Scope and Limits*, Simon and Schuster, Inc.

———, *An Inquiry into Meaning and Truth*, W.W. Norton and Co.

Jean-Paul Sartre, *Being and Nothingness*, Philosophical Library.

———, *Existentialism*, Philosophical Library.

———, *Existentialism and Human Emotions*, Philosophical Library.

Harold O. Soderquist, *The Person and Education*, Charles E. Merrill Books, Inc.

Jonas F. Soltis, *An Introduction to the Analysis of Educational Concepts*, Addison-Wesley.

C.E. Spearman, *The Creative Mind*, Appleton-Century.

P. Tillich, *The Courage to Be*, Yale University Press.

E.P. Torrance, *Education and the Creative Potential*, University of Minnesota Press.

———, *Guiding Creative Talent*, Prentice-Hall.

G. Watts, *The Art of Thought*, Franklin Watts.

A.N. Whitehead, *Adventures of Ideas*, New American Library.

———, *The Aims of Education*, New American Library.

———, *The Concept of Nature*, University of Michigan Press.

———, *Modes of Thought*, Macmillan.

C.S. Whiting, *Creative Thinking*, Reinhold.

John Wild, *The Challenge of Existentialism*, Indiana University Press.

Colin Wilson, *Introduction to the New Existentialism*, Houghton Mifflin Co.